T0196165

Brain Workout
Variety Puzzles to Boost Your Memory and Brainpower

iUniverse books may be ordered through booksellers or by contacting:

iUniverse
1663 Liberty Drive
Bloomington, IN 47403
www.iuniverse.com
1-800-Authors (1-800-288-4677)

ISBN: 978-1-4759-5705-1 (sc)
ISBN: 978-1-4759-5716-7 (hc)

Printed in the United States of America

iUniverse rev. date: 12/06/2012

Brain Workout

Variety Puzzles to Boost Your Memory and Brainpower

G. R. Roosta

iUniverse, Inc.
Bloomington

Brain Workout

Variety Puzzles to Boost Your
Memory and Brainpower

G. R. Roosta

iUniverse, Inc.
Bloomington

Brain Workout
Variety Puzzles to Boost Your Memory and Brainpower

iUniverse books may be ordered through booksellers or by contacting:

iUniverse
1663 Liberty Drive
Bloomington, IN 47403
www.iuniverse.com
1-800-Authors (1-800-288-4677)

ISBN: 978-1-4759-5705-1 (sc)
ISBN: 978-1-4759-5716-7 (hc)

Printed in the United States of America

iUniverse rev. date: 12/06/2012

Acknowledgments

I would like to express my sincere gratitude to many people who have made their contributions to the successful publication of this book. My special thanks go to Manfred Klein, Samuel Goldstein, Writ Large, Galdino Otten, Didik Pratikno, Didik Pratikno, Christophe Feray, Peter Wiegel, Dieter Steffmann, Dan Tingler, Brian Kent, Helen Duggan, Peter Slingsby, Ankokukoubou, Helen (pacific.net.au), Laura Cervera (nextiadesign.com), Steve Lundeen, and Speak Easy Inc. (speakeasy.org) for their permission to use their dingbat fonts in the present book's illustrations. I would also like to thank George Nedeff (Editorial Consultant), Victoria K. (Editor), and Hope Davis (Coordinator) at iUniverse, the publisher of the book. Finally, I would like to thank my older daughter, Parmis, for reviewing and checking the puzzles of the book, and to appreciate the support provided by my wife, Mozhgan, and my younger daughter, Paris.

Introduction

We can improve our brainpower considerably. This improvement happens by strengthening and making new connections between the neurons of our brain. More connections and stronger connections boost our brainpower and strengthen our performance on mental and physical activities. More precisely, stronger and more connections between neurons boost the cognitive functions of the brain, such as memory, attention, and reasoning. A brain with better cognitive functioning will have a higher capacity to learn and process; this fact in turn may mean a more "intelligent" brain.

Studies have shown that puzzles, and mental exercises in general, improve brainpower by stimulating the diverse regions of our brain, by stimulating creativity, imagination, and analytical, rational, and logical areas. This type of stimulation is one of the main ways to strengthen the existing connections between neurons and produce new connections. In many sources for brainpower improvement, the analogy has been made that as gymnasts can enhance their performance by more training and practice, people can enhance their brainpower by mental gymnastics provided by puzzles and brain games.

Using this book, which contains 220 puzzles and brain games, you can improve your mental functions, including memory, attention, speed, problem solving, and the verbal, numerical, and spatial capabilities of your brain, while entertaining yourself. The puzzles and games in this book are developed along a variety of different themes and styles and range in difficulty level and challenge. You will find it interesting and easy to complete in a fairly short time rather than a boring mental-exercise book that readers never complete.

Even though this book is primarily designed to challenge you in different ways in order to improve your memory and your brain aptitudes and abilities, it is also intended as a fun and entertaining collection to use at your leisure.

To get better results toward the book's primary targets, you may want to solve its puzzles and perform the exercises on a regular daily schedule, accomplishing at least ten items a day. In order to improve your brainpower with this book, the most important factor for a tangible achievement is that each puzzle and game should be accomplished within the time limit indicated; for example, if you are asked to solve a puzzle in thirty seconds, then you should diligently try to solve it in no more than thirty seconds. Please note that if you conscientiously try but cannot solve a puzzle in the given time, you should not consider this a failure but still a gain, as the brain has exercised a challenge by trying its best, and that makes it stronger.

Puzzles and Mental Games

1

Place the following fifteen letters in this star to form five 5-letter words all starting with S.

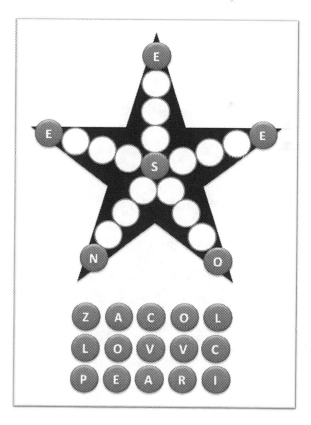

The numbers 1 to 9 are arranged in five overlapping squares where the total of the numbers in each square is fourteen. Can you rearrange these numbers so that the total of the numbers in each square is thirteen?

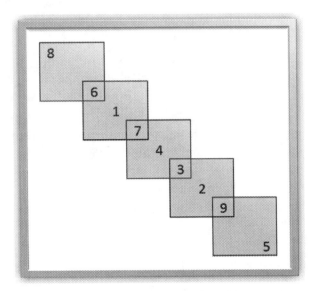

When the scrambled bird names listed below are unscrambled and placed along the horizontal rows, the letters in the dark boxes will spell out another bird name.

1. ORCNOD
2. LWLDAGA
3. DIRFRBUS
4. TRARSTED
5. IHCEWRDOT
6. OLNLOISBP
7. TTHHNAUC
8. HLOREVES

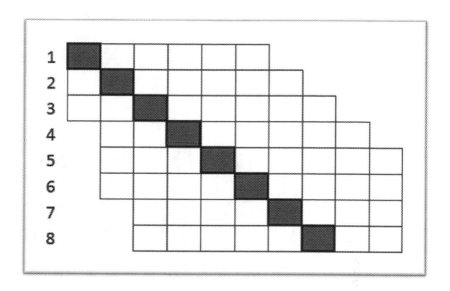

In the following puzzle, the numbers 1 to 9 are replaced with nine symbols. Can you identify what value should replace the question mark?

$$\Omega + \lambda - \Delta + \pi = 10$$
$$+ \quad + \quad + \quad +$$
$$\psi + \Phi - \Theta + \Sigma = 12$$
$$- \quad - \quad + \quad +$$
$$\mu + \Omega - \Delta - \pi = 5$$
$$+ \quad - \quad - \quad +$$
$$\psi - \Theta - \Phi + \Sigma = 0$$
$$= \quad = \quad = \quad =$$
$$? \quad\quad 8 \quad\quad 3 \quad\quad 20$$

In the following image, three girls are exactly the same. Can you identify them in twenty seconds?

Study the following picture for a moment.

Now, without referring to the above picture, validate the following statements:

a) The distance from A to C is longer than the distance from C to D.

b) The distance from A to B is longer than the distance from A to D.

Each cell of the following grid should be filled with one of the given symbols so that all the five symbols appear in each row and column. Can you complete this grid in five minutes?

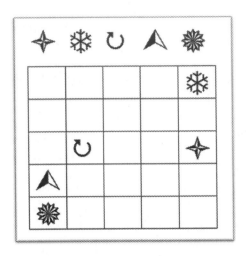

Study the grid below for thirty seconds.

Now, without looking at the above grid, identify which of the following pictures is a copy of the grid.

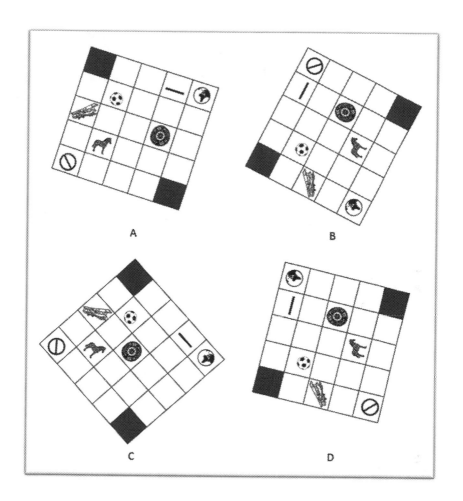

A

B

C

D

9

The *Word Sum Puzzle* (WSP) was first introduced by the author of this book in 2010. Here, you will solve ten WSPs.

A WSP is a word game that requires simple mathematical operations and vocabulary skills. The solution is always a single word that contains four or more letters.

A WSP has a clue and two or more hints, where the clue is a definition of the solution and each hint gives the sum of the numbers assigned to the first two letters, four letters, and so on of the solution. In an English WSP, the numbers assigned to the letters are the same as their order in the English alphabet (i.e., a = 1, b = 2, c = 3, ... z = 26 where capitals have the same values; e.g., A = 1 as a = 1). Let's try an example:

A curved part of a path:

   _ _ (7)

    _ _ _ _ (25)

The first line of this puzzle presents a clue. The other lines are the puzzle hints. This puzzle has two hints.

The first hint is the following:

   _ _ (7)

This hint indicates that the values of the first two letters of the answer make a sum of 7. Hence, the first two letters can be A & F (or F & A), B & E, C & D (or D & C).

The second hint is the following:

    _ _ _ _ (25)

It indicates that the values of the first four letters of the answer make a sum of 25. But based on the first hint, it is already known that the first two letters make a 7; therefore the third and fourth letters make a sum of 18. So they can be A & Q, B & P, C & O, D & N, E & M, I & I.

To solve the puzzle, the player should find which two pairs of letters discerned from these hints can make a word that means *"a curved part of a path."*

A & F + A & Q (NO)

A & F + B & P (NO)

...

B & E + D & N (YES)

The solution for this example is "bend."

Now try to solve the following ten WSPs.

a) Able to think or feel:

   _ _ (18)

   _ _ _ _ (51)

   _ _ _ _ _ _ (63)

   _ _ _ _ _ _ _ _ (99)

   _ _ _ _ _ _ _ _ _ (118)

b) The use of ridicule to show contempt:

   _ _ (9)

   _ _ _ _ (36)

   _ _ _ _ _ _ (64)

   _ _ _ _ _ _ _ (93)

c) Set of resources serving to prepare something:

   _ _ (22)

   _ _ _ _ (52)

   _ _ _ _ _ _ (81)

   _ _ _ _ _ _ _ (100)

_ _ _ _ _ _ _ _ _ (120)

d) A number of voters entitled to elect a representative:

_ _ (18)

_ _ _ _ (51)

_ _ _ _ _ _ (80)

_ _ _ _ _ _ _ _ (121)

_ _ _ _ _ _ _ _ _ _ (140)

_ _ _ _ _ _ _ _ _ _ _ _ (168)

e) Always:

_ _ (24)

_ _ _ _ (53)

_ _ _ _ _ _ (76)

f) Rivalry:

_ _ (18)

_ _ _ _ (47)

_ _ _ _ _ _ (72)

_ _ _ _ _ _ _ _ (101)

_ _ _ _ _ _ _ _ _ _ (125)

_ _ _ _ _ _ _ _ _ _ _ (139)

g) Pernicious:

_ _ (9)

_ _ _ _ (47)

_ _ _ _ _ _ (69)

_ _ _ _ _ _ _ _ (88)

_ _ _ _ _ _ _ _ _ _ (109)

_ _ _ _ _ _ _ _ _ _ _ _ (121)

h) Misunderstanding:

_ _ (22)

_ _ _ _ (42)

_ _ _ _ _ _ (74)

_ _ _ _ _ _ _ _ (97)

_ _ _ _ _ _ _ _ _ _ (110)

_ _ _ _ _ _ _ _ _ _ _ _ (143)

_ _ _ _ _ _ _ _ _ _ _ _ _ _ (167)

_ _ _ _ _ _ _ _ _ _ _ _ _ _ _ _ (181)

i) Thoughtless or heedless:

_ _ (23)

_ _ _ _ (41)

_ _ _ _ _ _ (74)

_ _ _ _ _ _ _ _ (87)

_ _ _ _ _ _ _ _ _ _ (110)

_ _ _ _ _ _ _ _ _ _ _ _ (131)

_ _ _ _ _ _ _ _ _ _ _ _ _ (136)

j) A proper occasion to progress:

_ _ (31)

_ _ _ _ (62)

_ _ _ _ _ _ (100)

_ _ _ _ _ _ _ _ (135)

_ _ _ _ _ _ _ _ _ _ (164)

_ _ _ _ _ _ _ _ _ _ _ (189)

10

In the following picture, each figure appears once and just two of them appear twice. You have thirty seconds to find the duplicates.

11

Pair off these three-letter fragments to form six cities each containing six letters.

ANK	ADH	FRE	OXF
SNO	BER	ARA	LAS
LIN	RIY	DAL	ORD

In ten minutes or less, find a path from the START to the END passing only through numbers that are *divisible by 6*. Note that there is only one solution for this numerical maze.

To help you find numbers divisible by 6 more quickly, here is a hint to remember and apply:

If the sum of the digits of a number is divisible by 3 *and* its last digit is even, then that number is divisible by 6. For example, 612 is divisible by 6, because the sum of its digits, nine (6 + 1 + 2 = 9), is divisible by 3, and its last digit, 2, is an even number.

START	78	312	872	730	800	148	640	76	146	158	86
652	88	546	444	684	842	190	682	118	188	116	562
742	812	160	652	336	830	178	552	108	420	184	676
106	176	104	550	816	164	92	360	112	852	848	196
190	766	252	162	660	118	188	948	136	480	932	790
178	790	834	214	706	142	804	870	124	192	562	442
184	606	858	184	456	306	528	189	130	204	142	212
208	672	854	208	468	556	436	176	978	912	896	754
196	894	972	276	486	164	744	396	648	688	124	194
772	842	190	682	568	188	966	184	110	112	182	142
184	676	112	182	574	176	882	462	96	294	128	574
896	754	824	172	664	100	170	98	196	726	750	END

In this puzzle, there are twenty-five books that should be divided by five rectangles, each rectangle containing exactly five books without overlapping any adjacent rectangles. Can you draw the rectangles in fifteen seconds?

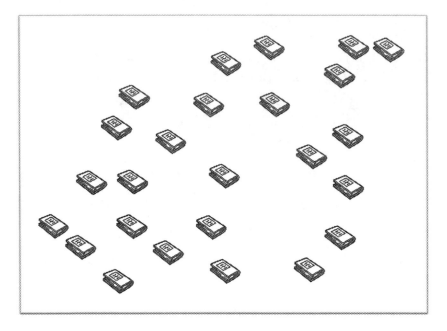

14

In the following figure, can you find which three crowns are identical in twenty seconds?

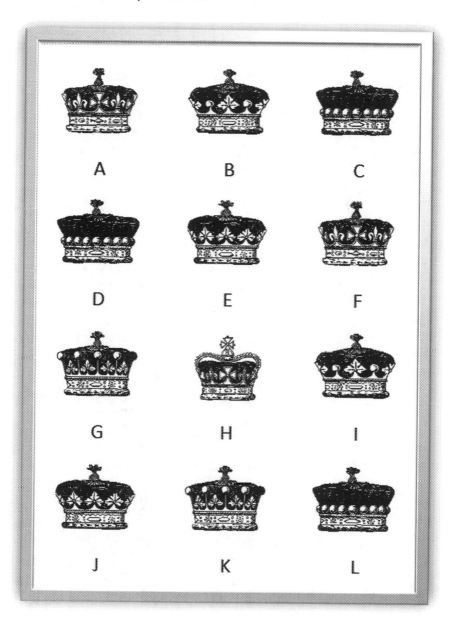

Starting from the center circle, move up, down, left, or right but not diagonally to find a city in the United States.

D	Q	N	Y	B	E	I	B	E	P	N
U	U	M	G	A	N	U	M	U	A	Y
M	F	X	C	E	R	T	C	M	D	E
H	E	A	B	E	W	M	A	N	A	F
K	C	T	E	O	O	D	I	H	P	J
E	D	O	V	R	I	N	B	L	O	E
M	C	P	H	S	N	C	S	I	B	H
Z	A	D	M	I	G	L	F	M	E	Y
B	E	L	B	O	B	V	E	Y	U	A
P	A	F	G	O	A	L	M	O	C	P
A	C	O	P	D	I	E	E	A	Y	F

Study the ornament inside the following oval for a moment.

Now, without looking at the above picture, can you find which of the following figures displays the same spatial illustration as the ornament?

The antonyms for the following five words are included in the figure below. Can you find them?

1. Wrangle
2. Chapfallen
3. Surcease
4. Machination
5. Feeble

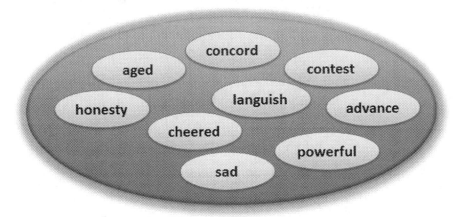

Look at the following picture, where one tile is missing. Can you find the missing piece?

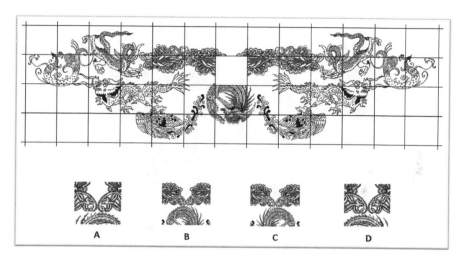

A   B   C   D

Can you travel from A to B by passing through all the white blocks only once each?

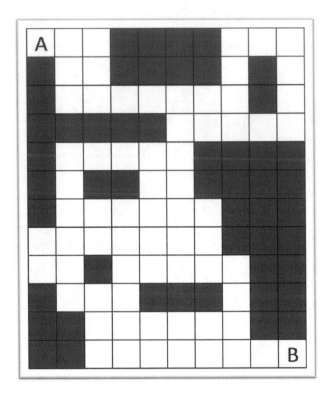

Each circle below contains a *circular word* that can be spelled by starting at the appropriate letter and moving clockwise or counterclockwise around the circle. Can you identify the words?

Note that a circular word is a word that ends with the same letters as its own starting letters (e.g., "emblem," which starts and ends with "em").

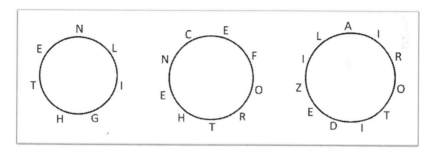

The following is an easy 5×5 *Futoshiki* puzzle. Place the numbers 1 to 5 in each row and column such that no number is repeated and the inequality constraints are followed.

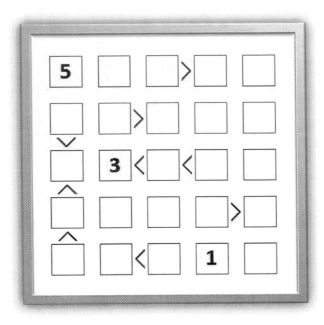

In this word search puzzle, the titles of ten award-winning novels are included. Can you find them?

```
H T S C T Q W T A H C C G Y H A X V H J
I N S C J H A P F S U N Y V F V Q J Z J
M A N G O N E D O W N N J N O V B U B X
Q B N X M Y R E E E V S I M L L T E Z P
W G M L Q J Y X D N Y K Y N I K K G C Y
C V N V A O C B O G G K F F I V I D W I
E R X D T H E B O N E P E O P L E I F N
G J Q F V Y L U F I Y O S P U G U R E R
E S Q M M S P O P P F B F L Z K N E V U
O Q E D Q M R Q X P W D O S N H U T L D
O A W L E U U X I I P H X M A Q G T H F
W H Y N P Q P N A H R T E H W D H I V Q
I J O Z T Q R E Z S O B N O G W N K C R
A Z S M S N O S S E L G N I H T A E R B
C R E P U Z L L P H N S S R Q I V V S A
X V N N U H O A M T E X E E Z Q M I U S
P W A T J W C F R H F O S V I X W L Z Z
Q V D A O R E H T A O F L H T B V O M E
Z Z V A U N H F L C H O B O G G O P Z U
D U W T J R T N I M B L Q Q T H O R K C
```

Breathing Lessons

Life of Pi

Olive Kitteridge

The Bone People

The Color Purple

The Edge of Sadness

Man Gone Down

The Shipping News

The Snow Queen

The Road

John buys a laptop that comes with a laptop bag. The total price is $678. When the store owner gives him the bag, he asks John if he can pay him and keep the empty bag. John asks how much he would pay for it. The store owner says the laptop costs $550 more than its empty bag. John accepts the deal. How much does John receive for the bag?

This is a maze. You should travel from the START block to the END block. You can go horizontally and vertically but not diagonally. In this maze, when you are on a letter, then your next move can be to an adjacent letter that comes after in the alphabetical order (e.g., from the letter P you can move to the letter R but not to the letter O). The exception is the letter Z, from which you can move only to the letter A. Note that you cannot cross your path.

START	G	F	D	L	G	K	U	L	J	D	J
M	O	A	G	I	M	A	Z	A	Q	R	L
Q	T	Z	A	N	G	I	K	U	T	Q	X
U	U	A	B	E	F	F	M	Z	B	A	T
A	J	H	Q	Q	C	I	P	N	O	M	M
N	M	V	P	R	A	N	S	G	F	L	O
X	P	R	U	W	Z	D	T	M	C	J	P
B	E	H	Z	D	A	M	V	P	I	K	K
O	W	I	S	L	F	A	Z	A	E	A	N
J	A	Z	T	H	C	H	W	R	H	Z	A
E	P	A	N	B	Q	R	T	V	W	X	W
P	Y	D	K	M	O	X	A	W	A	Z	END

You have fifteen seconds to solve this easy puzzle by linking the twelve circles without raising your pen. Note that you should not cross any other shapes and also that you cannot pass between two shapes more than once.

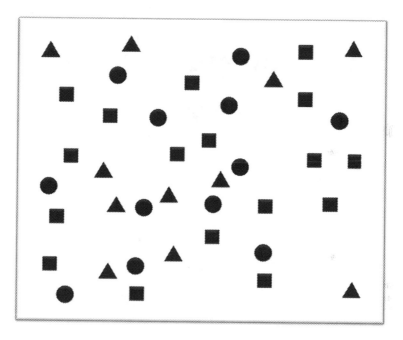

You have three minutes to make words from the following letters. Each letter should be used only once, each word should contain four letters or more, and you should try to make more words as much as you can during this three-minute period.

Hint: There are forty-four letters. To make the highest number of words, you may try to make eleven 4-letter words.

ARAYBACOEWFIGEHAINJOLMPOQEURDRDRNSTSTTEVIKYA

Use the numbers 1 to 9 to fill in the missing numbers. Note that each number is used once and that multiplication and division are performed prior to addition and subtraction.

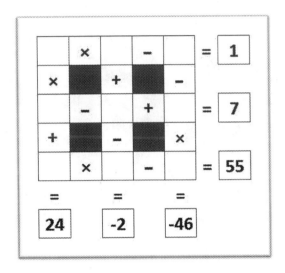

This is a fairly hard version of the previous puzzle. Use the numbers 1 to 25 to fill in the missing numbers. Remember that each number is used once and that multiplication and division are performed prior to addition and subtraction.

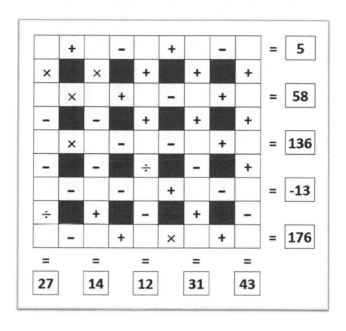

These are two identical dice in two different positions. By knowing that 5 is opposite 3, can you determine what number is opposite 4?

Can you divide the following dark area into eight lots with the same shape?

In the following equation there are nine squares that should contain numbers 1 to 9. Can you find the number of each square?

☐ + ((☐☐ - ☐) ÷ ☐) - ☐ - ☐ - ☐☐ = 0

Here you will solve ten *Word Trim Puzzles* (WTP). A WTP is a puzzle formed by a clue and a string of letters that includes the answer. To find the answer, you should trim the string (i.e., remove some letters from the start and the end of the string). Let's start with an example. This is a WTP:

To refuse abruptly:

lwoebalkpulze

To solve it, try to find an English word that means *"to refuse abruptly"* and that is inserted in the string *"lwoebalkpulze."* The answer is "balk," as shown in bold in the string "lwoe**balk**pulze." To detect "balk" you should trim "lwoe" from the start and "pulze" from the end of the string.

Note that in some strings of puzzles you may find more than one English word; however, only one of them is the correct answer. For example, in "lwoebalkpulze," you could find the English word "woe," but this word does not mean "to refuse abruptly."

Now try to solve the following WTPs:

a) Compendium:

  sfefrosummaryered

b) A person who undertakes a service without expectation of reward:

  equisvolunteergphy

c) A small old-world rodent that is intermediate in form and behavior between a mouse and a squirrel:

pfadormouseresthed

d) The environment where a plant or animal naturally lives:

moquirhabitataxgray

e) A fortified place:

powerosstrongholdfleweler

f) A living being:

meritcreaturetive

g) Relating to, or occurring in the night:

volunocturnaleast

h) The quality of having different forms:

diffevarietylare

i) A row of bushes or shrubs forming a hedge:

undercozihedgerowallerty

j) To make a thin shallow cut:

scrappiscratchered

In the following figure can you find which four figures are identical in thirty seconds?

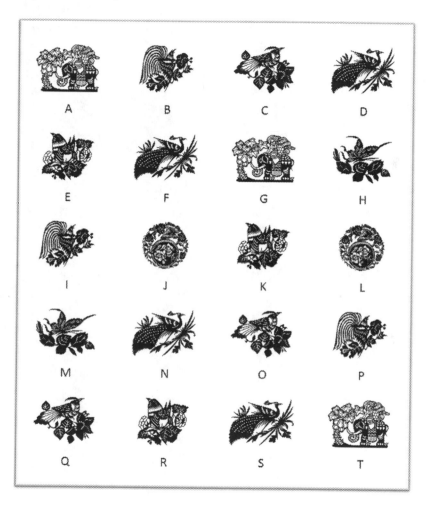

34

Try to answer the following question in no more than thirty seconds:

It takes John six hours to do a job, but Todd does the same job in four hours and Peter in only three hours. In half a day—twelve hours—how many such jobs could they do together?

35

Peter sold ninety-one printers during a seven-day sale. Each day he sold three more printers than he did on the previous day. Can you find how many printers were sold on the third day?

One of these figures is different from the rest. Can you spot the difference in thirty seconds?

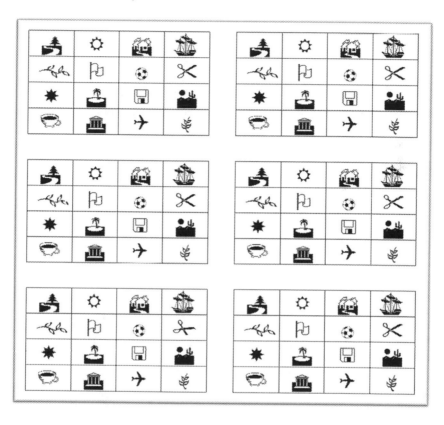

You have ten minutes to fit the given numbers into the following grid.

Across:

68	918	1609	971234
32	752	9805	864759
20	863	2473	869543
19	101	4087	142768
	276	6819	
	191	9062	
		3264	
		1807	

Down:

90	378	1014	20391
79	617	5294	21890
70	167	3721	80818
63	245	9803	98021
80	752		69692
16	647		41012
	645		
	369		

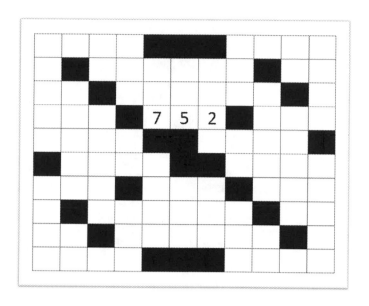

Eight numbers are placed on the following circle. Try to find the pattern and identify the missing number.

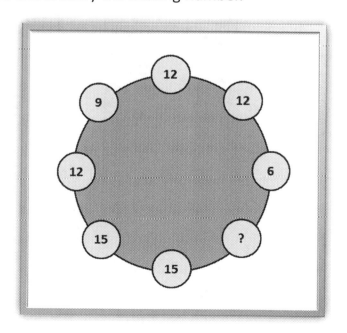

Study this picture for a moment.

In which of the following figures, if a section inside it rotates, would the above picture be found?

A

B

C

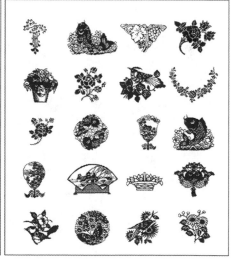

D

As a memory challenge, study the following picture for two minutes.

Now, without referring to the above picture, can you find which of the following figures appears more frequently than others?

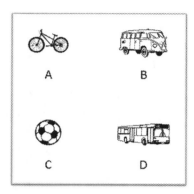

In two minutes, can you form two sets of three identical cars from the following picture?

42

The first five terms of the series 1, 2, 3, 4, 5, add up to 15. Can you find what five terms of another series add up to 18?

43

In each horizontal row, which are the two synonyms?

a)	Authorize	Scrutinize	Agonize	Audit	Intervene	Prohibit
b)	Accuse	Baffle	Convey	Endure	Eliminate	Transmit
c)	Quidnunc	Wrangler	Kinky	Sorcerer	Yenta	Precarious
d)	Excruciation	Misconception	Beatitude	Heliolatry	Harrow	Machination
e)	Lumpen	Inflexible	Anguish	Versatile	Adaptable	Proximity

44

Use the following list of twenty-five lakes in the United States to complete this clue-less crossword grid.

Austin	Crescent	Pillsbury
Bankson	Greeson	Saylorville
Barbee	Hartwick	Selawik
Blackshear	Istokpoga	Waconda
Browns	Kissimmee	Washington
Candlewood	Lurleen	Wawasee
Chesuncook	Manitou	Wedowee
Clinton	Naknek	Williamstown
Coralville		

In the following maze, try to connect A to B in five minutes.

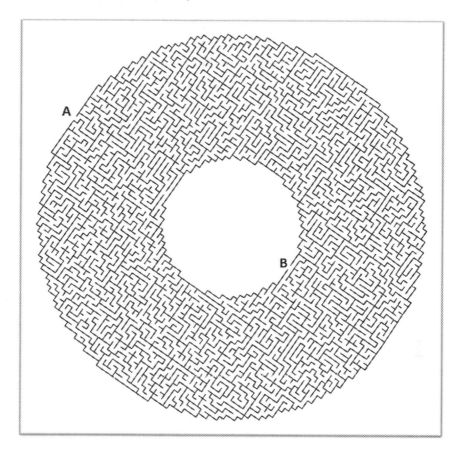

The following is a *Hitori* puzzle. You should eliminate numbers by filling in the squares in order such that the remaining cells do not contain duplicate numbers in either a row or a column. Note that your filled cells can be diagonally adjacent but not horizontally and vertically.

5	2	5	6	7	6	1	3	4
8	2	9	2	2	7	4	2	3
9	4	2	2	5	3	6	7	8
5	3	1	1	8	6	9	1	7
3	7	6	6	4	8	3	1	5
6	5	1	4	3	4	7	4	8
3	6	5	7	7	2	5	4	2
1	7	7	3	2	6	8	8	9
7	9	2	5	6	4	8	8	6

This is another easy memory challenge. Study the following figure for one minute.

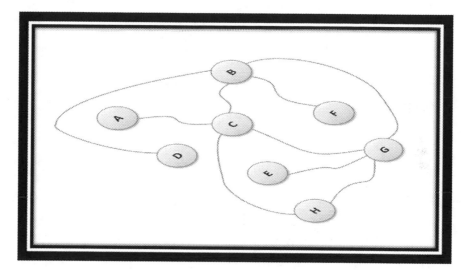

Now, from memory, validate the following statements by saying True or False:

a) A is connected to F

b) B is connected to H

c) B is connected to D

d) E is connected to F

e) A is connected to C

What number should replace the question mark?

1, 1, ?, 3, 5,

Hint: The above series of numbers presents a *Fibonacci sequence*.

Fibonacci (1170–1250), one of the leading mathematicians of the Middle Ages, is famous today because of this sequence.

John buys a used car for $2,000 (no tax). He pays in cash with a certain number of $1 bills, fifteen times as many $5 bills, a certain number of $10 bills, and three times as many $100 bills. How many bills of each kind does John use to pay for the car?

A *word scramble* is a word puzzle game that provides you with a group of jumbled letters to unscramble to make a real word. As an example, if you get the letters "TBES," you may unscramble them to detect the word "BEST."

A *two-dimensional word scramble* puzzle has two steps. In the first step you solve a couple of regular word scramble puzzles and identify the original words. In the second step you rearrange a given set of letters from these original words to discover the final word.

Now try to solve this two-dimensional word scramble puzzle:

There are seven 7-letter words as follows. Unscramble them and then take the middle letter of each word to make the final answer of this puzzle.

1. WEELYJR
2. YWDKOER
3. TSYMERY
4. OREOTSR
5. TEFNEBI
6. FIRLACY
7. SENSTFA

There are five positive whole numbers indicated by v, w, x, y, and z. We know that x is an odd number and:

$$v + w = 9$$

$$w + x = 5$$

$$x + y = 3$$

$$y + z = 5$$

Can you find these numbers?

In each horizontal row, only two words are synonyms. Can you find them?

a) VEXATIOUS, GREGARIOUS, INCONGRUOUS, ESOTERIC, GALLING

b) INSIPID, EREMITE, EXIGUOUS, ANCHORITE, AGELAST

c) DECLAIM, HALE, BESTOW, CONTRIBUTE, BIFURCATE

d) SOBRIQUET, CORMORANT, EPITHET, HOMAGE, HOODLUM

e) EXTEMPORE, INEFFABLE, INDESCRIBABLE, INDISPENSABLE, SLUGABED

Move through this maze to collect one hundred points. Pass each way or junction only once. Two arrows indicate your points of entry and exit.

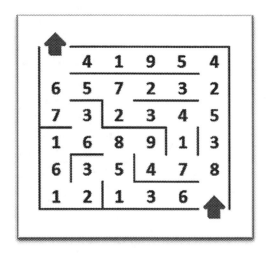

54

In the following figure, identify the values of x and y such that:

a) The sum of the numbers inside the circle must be greater than any of the sums of numbers inside the heart, the diamond, and the triangle.

b) The sum of the numbers inside the rectangle must be thirty-six units less than the total of the numbers inside the circle, the heart, the diamond, and the triangle.

c) Both x and y should be divisible by 5.

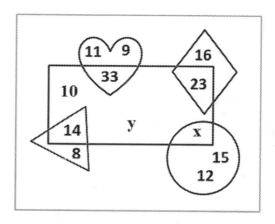

Four words related to gardening have been written in a row with neither spaces nor vowels. What are these four words?

PRNNGSLWDRSCP

Study the two figures inside the squares on the following wall for a moment.

Now, without looking at the above wall, can you find which of the following pictures displays the same spatial illustration as the two figures?

A

B

C

D

Study this picture for thirty seconds.

Now, without referring to the above picture, identify which three objects appear most often.

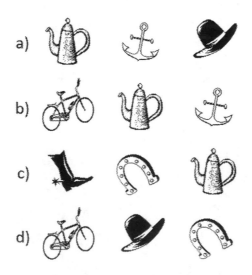

In the following figure, determine the connection between the letters and the numbers, and then identify which number should replace the question mark.

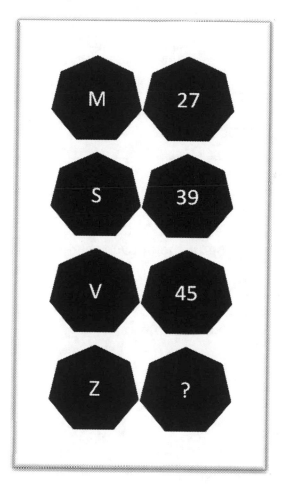

Here is a table where fifty bird names are listed. Review the table for no more than three minutes.

Woodpecker	Bittern	Eider	Grosbeak	Owl
Avocet	Egret	Willet	Gadwall	Flamingo
Flicker	Vulture	Blackbird	Finch	Pheasant
Sparrow	Bobwhite	Flycatcher	Vireo	Swallow
Chickadee	Crow	Gannet	Albatross	Dove
Oriole	Yellowhammer	Goldeneye	Cardinal	Grackle
Longspur	Grebe	Ovenbird	Scoter	Condor
Parrot	Oystercatcher	Siskin	Coot	Grouse
Killdeer	Crane	Heron	Cuckoo	Hummingbird
Curlew	Ibis	Weaver	Dipper	Dowitcher

Now, without looking at the above table, from your memory write five bird names all starting with G; note that the bird names should be from the table.

In this word search puzzle, the capitals of twenty countries are included. Can you find them?

```
R T L L A Q U O M U S A P C E F N D T A
A A J S T P L Y U U Y Y U H L D J S K C
R S U F A H L W R R H D J H L A T A N F
R H B B U C H A R E S T O G I C H K B J
E K L B A Y M M G A O E S H V D D A Q W
B E J F M W R X V I D R F A E D U Z O E
N N A D T R A V K I C C N G R W U H W S
A T N V Z S Z T V A D U N B B A K F T B
C U A U T R E E T L T W G R I R J O L U
Y D L Y J S T P M O O H S E L J C E X P
O V I R A N A N A T N A M L T K D Y V S
T Y U N O O U I E D W W D A H Z C X B O
K S L M K P M E R T U Z J O N R T F J C
A N A V A H R B O P V B L A B D K R C L
Y L W Y D F A X N O B M J N V W U J S A
H E L S I N K I A L O T L W N K B G U Q
M Z X M G W M O R F P V I Y R Y D F U Y
O B H K P X Z V H K V R R I A O W J H V
F C O U N V L N E D O U F G A G E K U L
P K N P A E B D T Y V A S L E S S U R B
```

Antananarivo	Canberra	Kathmandu	Sarajevo
Bangkok	Dhaka	Libreville	Stockholm
Brussels	Freetown	Ljubljana	Tashkent
Bucharest	Havana	Montevideo	Tegucigalpa
Budapest	Helsinki	Ottawa	Tehran

This is a maze. You should travel from the START block to the END block. You can go horizontally and vertically but not diagonally. In this maze, when you are on a number, your next move can only be to a higher adjacent number (e.g., from 5 you can move to 7 but not to 3). Note that you cannot cross your path.

START	1	4	13	9	6	16	28	29	15	16	19
2	7	6	1	28	29	30	31	34	35	36	20
4	5	16	26	26	19	4	5	18	10	37	15
7	6	17	33	24	23	45	43	41	40	38	5
9	7	18	17	23	21	48	40	13	20	12	18
11	8	17	19	22	17	49	48	55	36	63	12
20	9	7	14	21	13	51	44	67	68	70	22
19	10	3	16	19	15	55	67	66	3	73	39
23	11	13	8	18	17	57	62	64	6	75	49
5	12	18	10	17	16	8	52	8	87	79	78
11	13	14	15	16	15	18	77	66	77	86	88
18	5	20	14	14	13	74	99	83	84	75	END

The right-side list contains synonyms for the words listed at left. Can you connect the words that are synonyms?

didactic	visceral
misanthropic	pretentious
splanchnic	instructive
grandiose	pertinacious
tenacious	cynical

In the following puzzle, the numbers 1 to 9 are replaced with nine symbols. Can you identify what value should replace the question mark?

$$\Omega + \lambda + \Theta - \Delta + \Sigma = 23$$
$$-\quad -\quad -\quad -\quad -$$
$$\Delta + \mu + \Sigma + \lambda - \Omega = 5$$
$$+\quad +\quad +\quad +\quad +$$
$$\Theta + \psi + \pi + \Omega - \Phi = 20$$
$$-\quad -\quad -\quad -\quad -$$
$$\Phi - \pi + \mu + \psi - \Delta = 5$$
$$=\quad =\quad =\quad =\quad =$$
$$8\quad 2\quad 5\quad 4\quad ?$$

In the following figure, can you find which four figures are identical in thirty seconds?

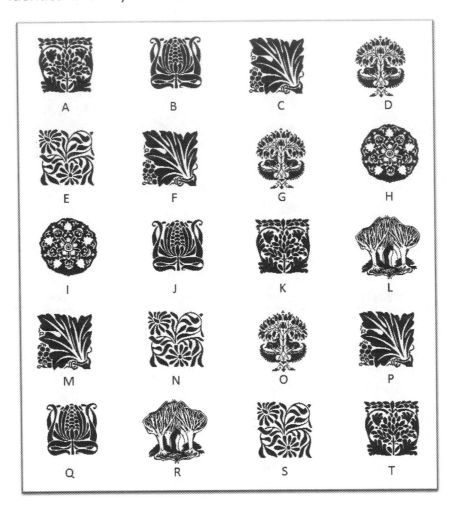

One of these figures is different from the rest. Can you spot the difference in a minute?

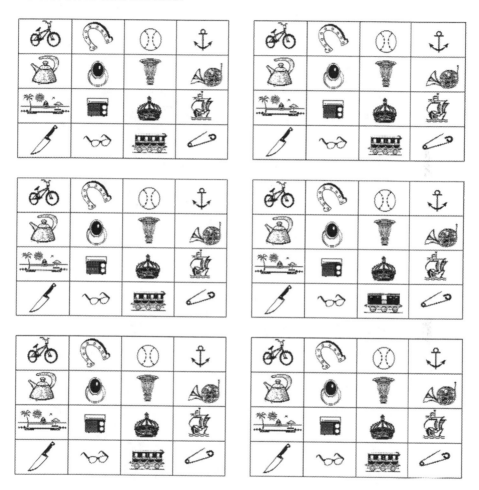

In no more than three minutes, find out which of the following 3×3 grids of letters should replace the question mark.

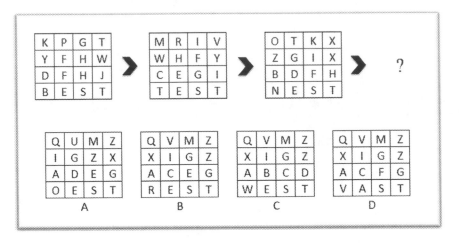

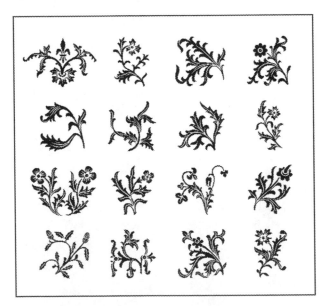

Study this picture for a moment.

In which of the following figures, if a section inside it rotates, can the above picture be found?

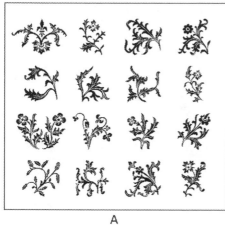

A

B

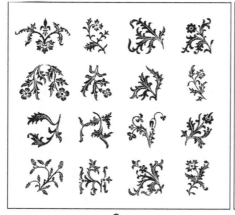

C

D

This is a visual Sudoku. You should fill in the grid so that every row, column, and 3×3 region contains the various figures exactly once.

In twenty seconds, can you find which two pictures are exactly alike?

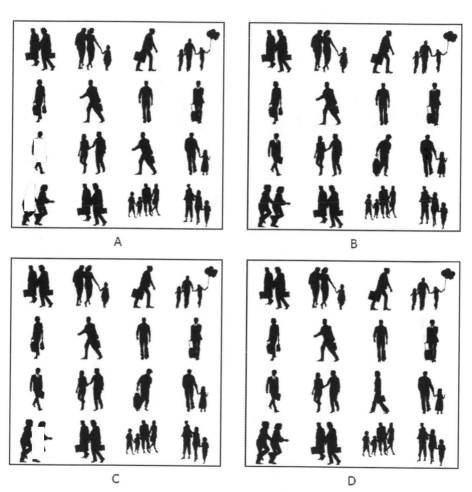

A

B

C

D

Try to keep these four items in your mind for twenty seconds; spend only five seconds on each.

Now identify which of the following four pictures contains all the four items.

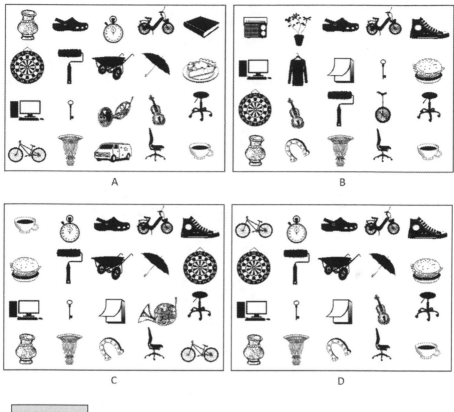

The digits of two numbers are scrambled as:

28293
76845

Can you unscramble them by knowing that one number is twice as large as the other?

You have twenty seconds to solve this puzzle by linking the twelve circles without raising your pen. Note that you should not cross any other shapes and also that you cannot pass between two shapes more than once.

Use the following list of twenty-five countries to complete this clue-less crossword grid.

Albania	Finland	Liechtenstein
Bangladesh	Germany	Paraguay
Belgium	Guatemala	Romania
Bulgaria	Honduras	Singapore
Cameroon	Indonesia	Swaziland
Colombia	Jamaica	Tanzania
Croatia	Kazakhstan	Turkmenistan
Denmark	Lebanon	Zimbabwe
Estonia		

Concatenate any three-digit number with itself (e.g., for 835 it would be 835835). Divide it by 7.

The remainder will be zero.

Example: For 235, you would have 235235, where 235235 divided by 7 will be 33605 with 0 as the remainder.

Now divide the quotient by 11. The remainder will be zero.

For the above example, 33605 divided by 11 will be 3055 with 0 as the remainder.

Again, divide the new quotient by 13. The remainder will be zero.

In the example, 3055 divided by 13 will be 235 and the remainder will be 0. Note that 235 is the original number of this example.

In summary:

235

235235 (concatenated by itself)

235235 ÷ 7 = 33605 (remainder is zero)

33605 ÷ 11 = 3055 (remainder is zero)

3055 ÷ 13 = 235 (remainder is zero and 235 is the original number)

As another example; take 743:

743

743743 (concatenated by itself)

743743 ÷ 7 = 106249 (remainder is zero)

106249 ÷ 11 = 9659 (remainder is zero)

9659 ÷ 13 = 743 (remainder is zero and 743 is the original number)

The reason is as follows:

$7 \times 11 \times 13 = 1001$

and multiplying 1001 by any three-digit number will be like concatenating it with itself (e.g., $100 \times 1001 = 100100$, or $532 \times 1001 = 532532$).

Hence, any number obtained by concatenating a 3-digit number with itself can be divided by 1001, and as 1001 is equal to $7 \times 11 \times 13$, it can be divided by 7, 11, and 13.

By knowing the above fact, in a minute, out of the following numbers, find four that are divisible by 13.

a) 713700

b) 845548

c) 145158

d) 987978

e) 426526

f) 469456

g) 363350

Place the following groups of letters into the ovals to form a chain of words so that a six-letter English word is formed when an oval is paired up with the next one.

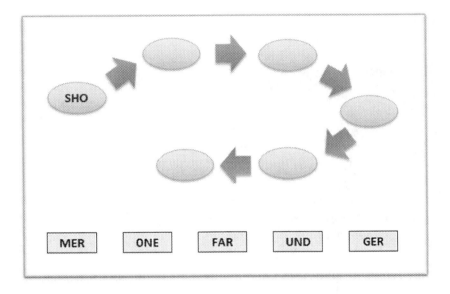

SHO

MER   ONE   FAR   UND   GER

You have thirty seconds to identify which figure is different from the others.

A

B

C

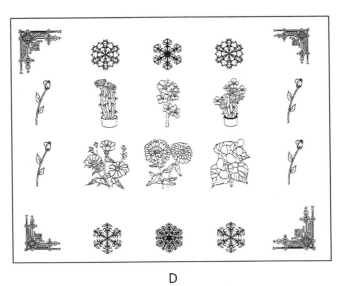

D

Find a ten-letter word in the grid below. This word starts with TR as highlighted in bold. Each next letter must have an edge in common with the previous letter.

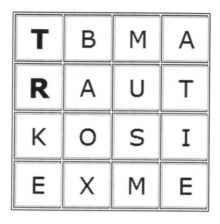

What two numbers complete this pattern?

In the following puzzle, starting from any letter, trace out a fourteen-letter English word by going along the lines without crossing any letter more than once.

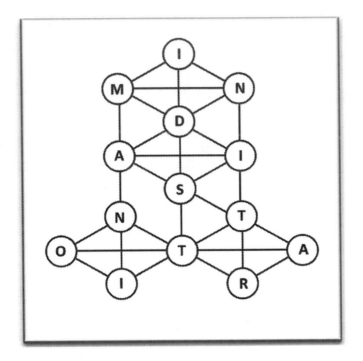

In a game of eleven players lasting for ninety minutes, four reserves alternate equally with each player; it means that all players, including the reserves, play for the same length of time. For how long does each player play?

Study the following patterns for one minute and remember the numbers assigned to each.

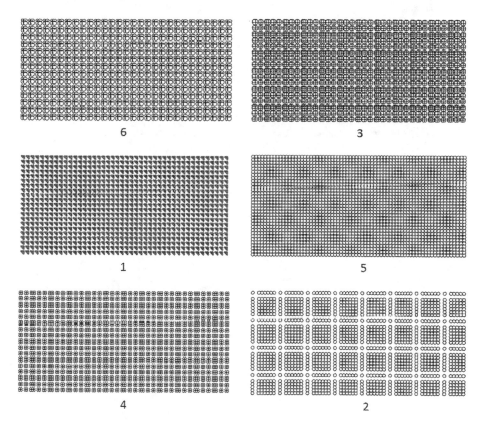

Without looking at the patterns, follow the scenario below and answer the question from your memory.

The number assigned to each pattern on the left side is swapped with the number of the pattern at its right.

Can you say what the current number of the pattern shown below is?

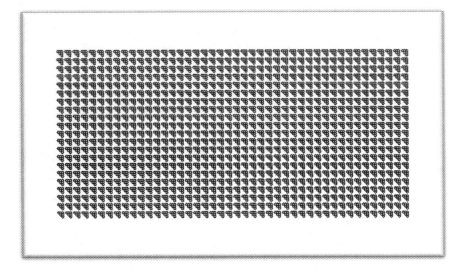

Which four butterflies are identical? Can you find them in one and a half minutes?

The *Wording Digit Puzzle* (WDP) was first introduced by the author of this book in 2010. Here you will solve ten WDPs.

A WDP is a word game that requires both logical and vocabulary skills. The solution is always a single word that should be inferred from a clue and a hint.

A WDP has a clue and one hint, where the clue is a meaning for the solution and the hint is a number presenting the solution.

Let's try an example.

Clue: Difficulty or failure in the alimentary canal in changing food into absorptive nutriment:

Hint: 1591997520941414

Solution:

Step 1. Remember that the digit(s) for each letter are the same as the order of the letter in the English alphabet (i.e., a = 1, b = 2, c = 3, d = 4, e = 5, y = 25, and z = 26).

Step 2. Try to find out some letters that can be inferred directly from the hint:

1591997520941414

In this number, 1591997520941414, the first "9" leads to an "i" because:

   a) in 1591997520941414, 59 is a number that is not assigned to any letter; numbers of letters range from 1 to 26 for "a" to "z."

b) in 1591997520941414, 91 is a number that is not assigned to any letter, so one of the letters of the answer is "i."

Again, the third "9" leads to an "i" because:

a) in 1591997520941414, 99 is greater than 26 and cannot be assigned to any letter.

b) in 1591997520941414, 97 is greater than 26 also and cannot be assigned to any letter.

Based on the above logic, find as many letters of the solution as possible.

Step 3. Try to find some logical hints. For example, if the first "9" in 1591997520941414 is an "i," then the first two digits of 1591997520941414 should lead to the following:

1 and 5 are an "a" and "e"

or

15 is an "o"

Step 4. With some letters that you found, refer to the clue— "Difficulty or failure in the alimentary canal in changing food into absorptive nutriment"—and find the answer, "indigestion":

9,14,4,9,7,5,19,20,9,15,14—indigestion

Now try to solve the following ten WDPs.

a) Created or formed by the imagination:

962092120915319

b) Contempt for the opinions of others and of what others value:

253191439139

c) Spreading rapidly through the system:

9215619122649

d) Any state of great happiness:

520412129520

e) To entertain:

916181941520

f) Heady; reckless:

15181251512684

g) Deviating from the normal form or standard type:

18138188165153915205

h) Figuratively oppressed; subjugated:

234151414415185420

i) A physical, mental, or moral weakness:

91320618914259

j) To reduce to ashes:

35991141452018

In thirty seconds, can you form two sets of three identical insects from the following picture?

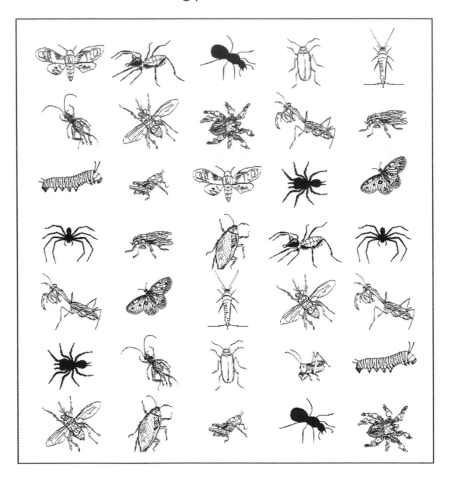

In the following figure, can you find which four ships are identical in twenty seconds?

What number should replace the question mark?

52   48   56   40   72   ?

Using two straight lines, divide this circle into four pieces, each of which contains numbers that add up to twenty-five.

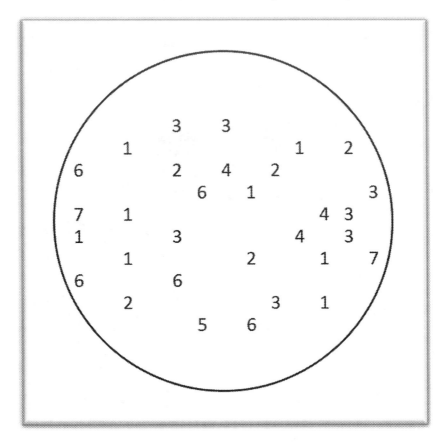

88

Can you connect A to B in just three minutes?

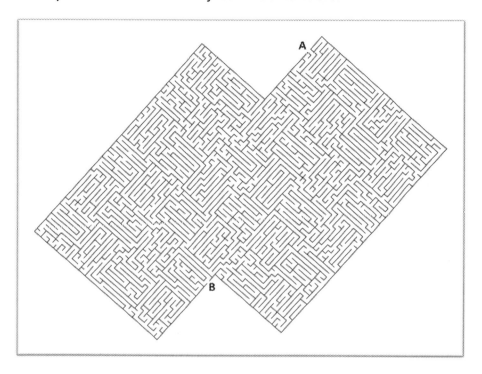

89

Find a word that fits in front of all the following endings.

- COCK
- BUCKLE
- TABLE
- STILE
- COAT

In ten seconds, can you find how many circles are located in the following figure?

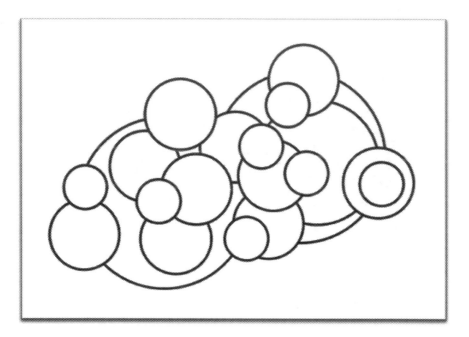

The following is a 7×7 Futoshiki puzzle. Place the numbers 1 to 7 in each row and column such that no number is repeated and the inequality constraints are followed.

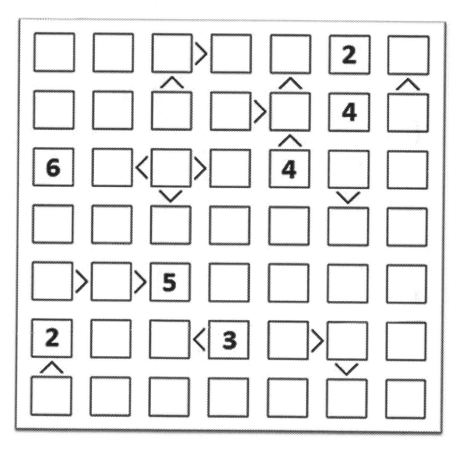

Inside the following pentagon, the black dot moves three places clockwise and the white dot moves two place counterclockwise at each stage. After how many stages will they be together in the same corner?

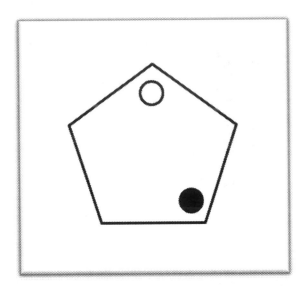

Fill in the next domino in the following sequence.

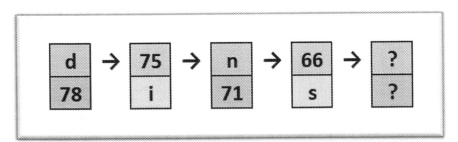

94

Two numbers are such that if the first gets 24 from the second they will be in the ratio 2 to 1, but if the second receives 33 from the first, their ratio will be 1 to 5. What are these two numbers?

95

Which letter will complete this word?

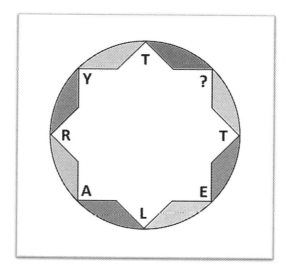

96

Which year does not confirm with the others?

    a) 1958

    b) 1955

    c) 1865

    d) 1856

This is a *Letstat* exercise. Study the following words for two minutes:

- opposite
- oral
- pop
- band
- gap
- load
- pend
- own
- node
- soap
- pray
- bag
- pet
- coat
- pin
- car
- pair
- port
- code
- order
- pick
- out
- boat
- pipe
- can
- name
- open
- boot

Now try to answer the following two questions. You should not see the list when answering the questions; however, if you feel that you did not pay enough attention the first time, feel free to review the list for one more minute and then come back to the questions.

a) What letter appears most often?

b) What letter is most used as the starting letter?

98

Which four-letter word can be placed at the start of this puzzle to form three 8-letter words?

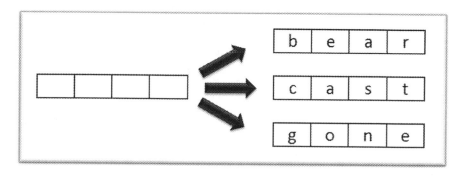

99

Use the eight operators below to complete the following two equations.

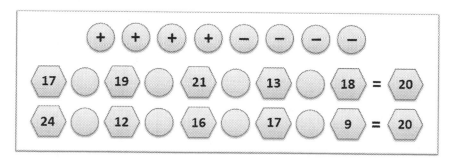

In two minutes, try to find one different detail in each picture.

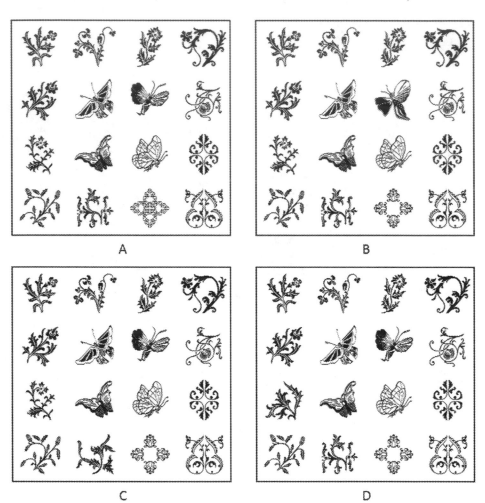

A

B

C

D

On this target, get a total of two hundred points with five arrows.

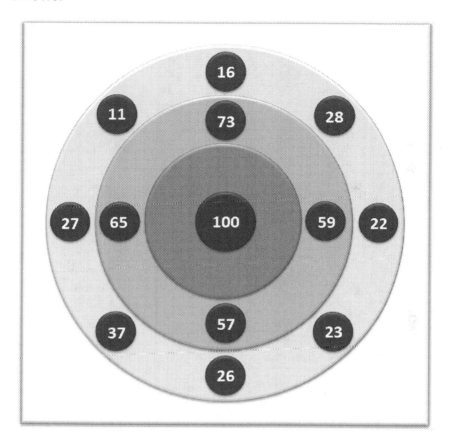

As a memory challenge, study the following picture for one minute.

Now, without looking at the above picture, can you find which of the following figures appears more frequently than the others?

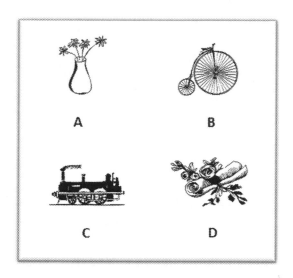

A

B

C

D

103

Which pattern comes next in this sequence?

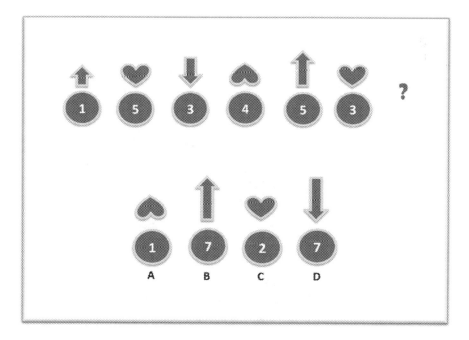

Divide this figure into eight parts of equal size such that each part contains one teapot.

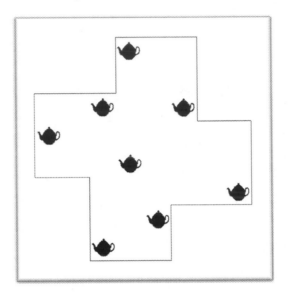

Which cube can be made by folding this figure?

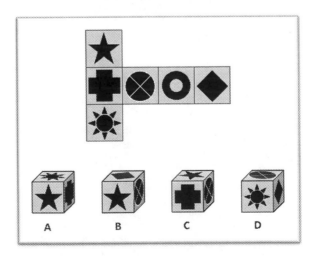

Reposition the following letters to form five words related to aircraft.

a) **ILAFIRO**

b) **ELTTERAIM**

c) **AAYDPLO**

d) **REILNAO**

e) **NEURIPLAQAD**

107

Which figure does not belong to the following group?

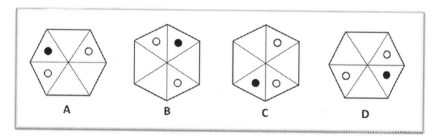

A   B   C   D

108

In thirty seconds determine which figure completes the series.

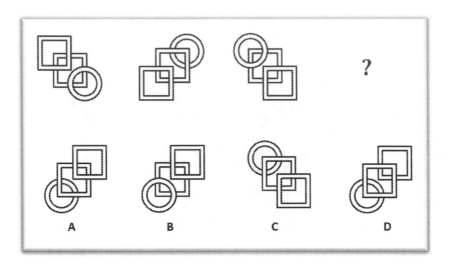

109

In the circles below, put the following letters in order to form a verb that means "to make famous forever."

110

What is the missing figure in the lower right corner?

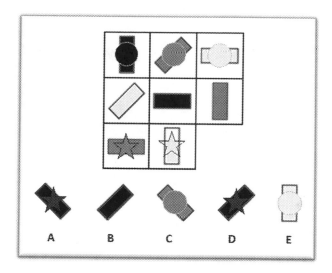

111

Study the following picture, which contains twenty shapes, for two minutes.

Now, without referring to the above picture, draw a circle around the five shapes in the picture below that are not included in the above one.

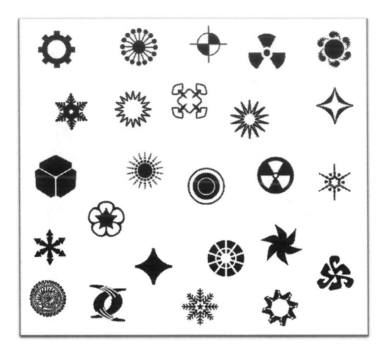

Which figure completes the series below?

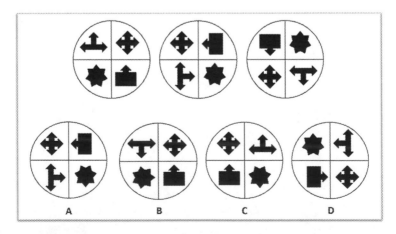

A   B   C   D

In each row of circles below, make one word with only the letters A, R, and T and those already placed.

Find the figure that logically follows the first three.

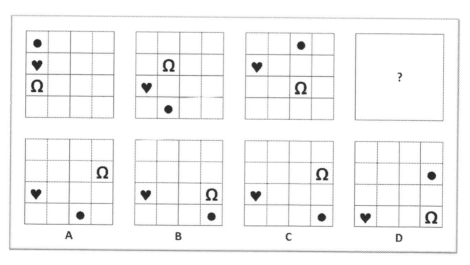

115

Draw a path from A to B through all the five rectangular caves, passing through each path only once.

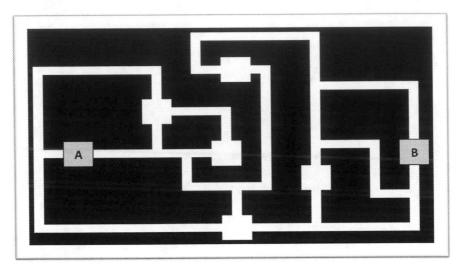

116

Can you find seven closed areas such that none of them is adjacent to another in any edge?

117

What is the total area covered by the columns?

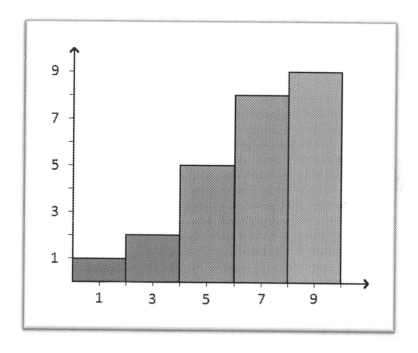

A) 48

B) 50

C) 52

D) 54

Reposition the following letters to form answers for the corresponding clues.

a)   Liturgical chanting:

a)   L I T N A C O N I A L T

b)   To divest of concern:

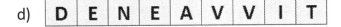

b)   I N S S E D E R T T I

c)   Having a large belly:

c)   M S O U I D B A O N

d)   Not yet well established:

d)   D E N E A V V I T

e)   Small European grebe:

e)   A K I C C B H D

119

Eliminate two bowling pins from this puzzle. Then divide the remaining ones into two groups of four pins such that the sum of the numbers of the two groups is the same.

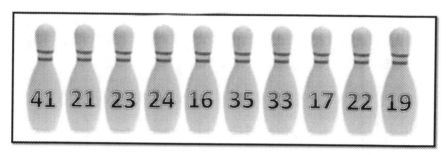

120

In a class, there are nine students with green eyes, eleven brunette students, and three students who are neither green-eyed nor brunette. If six students are green-eyed brunettes, how many students are in the class?

Which are the seven pieces that, when assembled, form a perfect square?

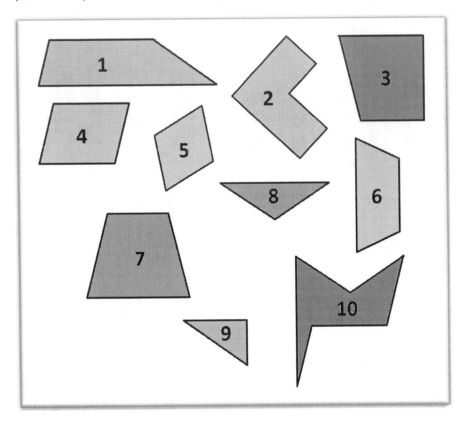

The letters of two synonymous nine-letter words are located in the following two blocks. As illustrated, these blocks have two letters in common. Can you find the two words?

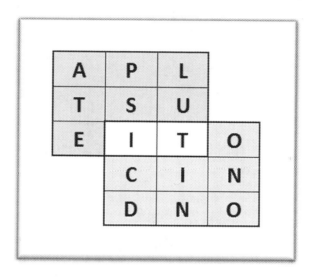

Study the following figure for a moment.

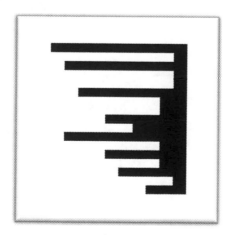

Which piece below forms a perfect square with the above figure?

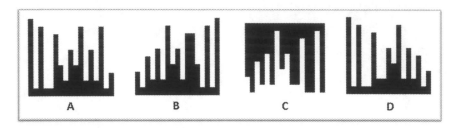

A   B   C   D

124

In the following puzzle, how many times can the small piece fit into the larger piece?

In order to water this flower, open the minimum number of valves to allow water to flow from the hydrant to the hose.

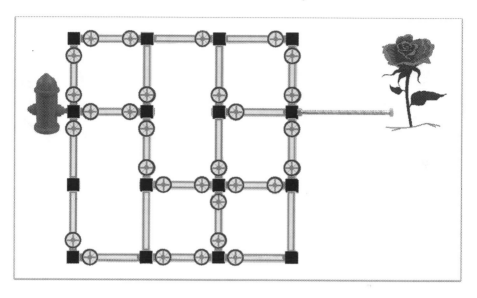

Find the word hidden in this grid. All the letters are used, and each letter is used only once.

Which number comes next in this sequence?

7 → 22 → 53 → 106 → 187 → ?

In this picture, the square displays the face of the stamp as illustrated below:

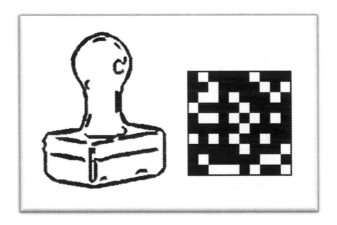

In thirty seconds identify which of the following four prints was created by the stamp.

Which letter completes the series?

A D H M S ?

Study the following three shapes for three minutes and then cover them.

Now, on the grid below where some elements are given, redraw only one of the above images, covering all the elements given.

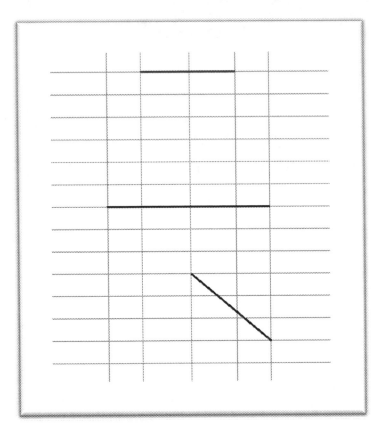

131

What are the letters that complete the series?

BY ?? DW EV

Which figure, A, B, C, or D, logically follows the series?

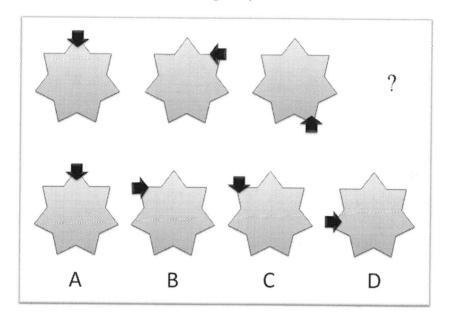

133

Determine the missing letter.

23(Z) 16(S) 15(R) 8(?)

Complete the following board of numbers.

11	15	14
14	13	13
12	11	?

Which number comes next in this sequence?

298, 292, 274, 238, 178, ?

Divide this figure into six parts of the same size such that each part contains one star.

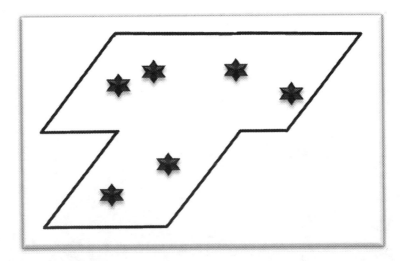

What are the two numbers that complete the series?

4, 9, 24, 69, ?, ?, 1824

138

What number should be placed at the center?

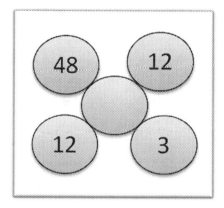

139

Which of the pieces shown in A through D form a perfect square with the figure below?

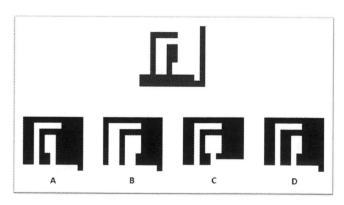

On this target, get a total of 270 points with four arrows.

Which number comes next in this sequence?

119 → 96 → 74 → 53 → ?

Find the word, the name of a plant, hidden in this grid. All letters are used once except one, which is used twice.

On this target, get a total of 540 points with four arrows.

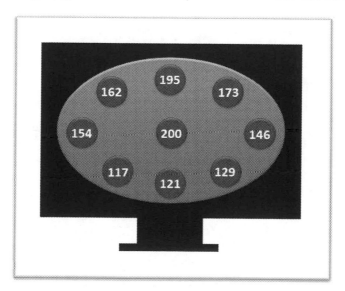

144

Can you complete the following table? In its four rows, four 10-letter English words should be located, all ending with "gate."

	m				g	a	t	e
	o				g	a	t	e
	o				g	a	t	e
	n				g	a	t	e

145

Which figure completes the series?

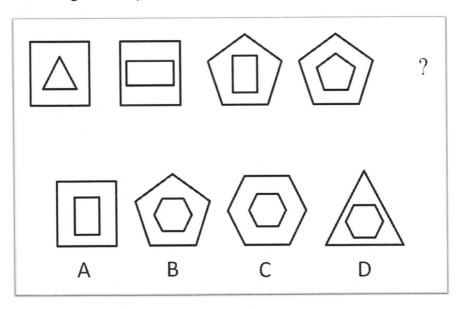

Divide this figure into six parts of the same size such that each part contains one star.

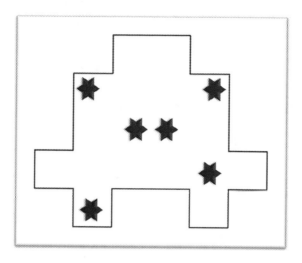

Which cube can be made by folding this figure?

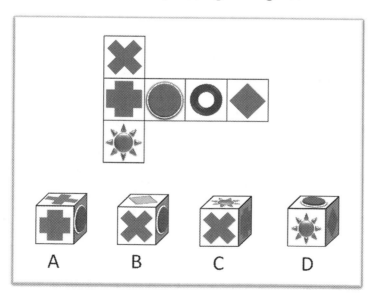

Which word completes the series?

SINGER, MACHINE, TRAVELER, BLISTERED,

A) SOLITARY

B) AGREEMENT

C) LEGISLATIVE

D) CONTIGUOUS

One figure does not belong to the following group; which one is it?

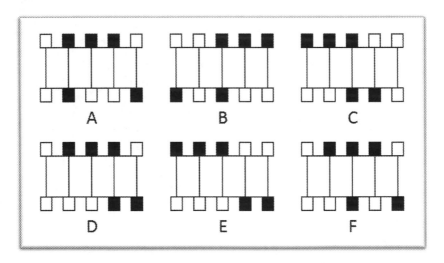

Which figure completes the series?

28	8	36
4	6	10
7	48	55

40	9	49
5	7	12
8	63	71

54	10	64
6	8	14
9	80	89

?

64	11	75
8	9	17
8	99	107

A

70	11	81
7	9	16
10	99	109

B

68	11	82
7	10	18
9	121	110

C

80	110	15
8	10	11
10	11	165

D

151

Each of the following series follows a different mathematical sequence. Can you deduce which number comes next?

A) 72   64   57   51   46   ?

B) 0   2   4   12   32   ?

C) 3   5   9   17   33   ?

D) 99   80   63   48   35   ?

E) 1   4   11   30   85   ?

F) 16   22   12   26   8   ?

152

A car leaves Vancouver for Seattle traveling at 60 miles an hour through a route of 150 miles. Another car leaves Seattle for Vancouver 20 minutes later traveling at 70 miles an hour through the same route. Where the cars meet, are they closer to Vancouver or Seattle?

A. Vancouver

B. Seattle

C. Same distance

153

A snail is at the bottom of a well fifty meters deep. Every day the snail climbs ten meters upward; however, at night it slides six meters back downward. How many days does it take until the snail reaches the top of the well?

a) Ten days

b) Eleven days

c) Twelve days

d) Thirteen days

154

Place the following groups of letters into the boxes to form a chain of words such that an English word is formed when each box is paired up with the next box.

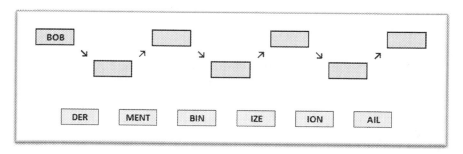

155

The first two scales are in balance. How many squares do you need to balance the third scale?

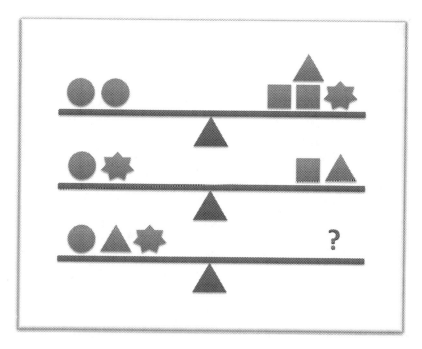

156

Reposition the following letters to unscramble five bird names.

CKEERDOWOP

MIFGNOLA

BIBLKRDAC

ANPASTHE

TWHOBIEB

157

This is a Letstat exercise. (You have done this exercise once in this book; can you remember what Letstat is about?)

Study the following words for two minutes.

- byte
- tiny
- bent
- rite
- bring
- fast
- puzzle
- take
- mend
- plug
- advice
- serve
- mind
- cable
- face
- indirect
- opaque
- rowel
- bottom

- invite
- tyrant
- quaint
- light
- fixture
- realist
- venus
- winglet
- prowl
- festival
- ledger

Now try to answer the following five questions. Note that a rough answer is better than no answer.

a) How many words were in the list?

b) Is the letter A used more often in the list or the letter T?

c) If you know that there are 160 letters used to make the list, can you roughly estimate in what percentage the letter E was used?

d) What three letters were used only once in the list?

e) What two letters were most used as the starting letter?

The antonyms for the five following words are located in the figure below. Can you find them?

1. Jocund
2. Chicanery
3. Propitious
4. Pecuniary
5. Vexatious

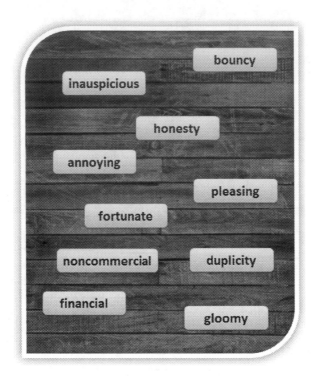

159

Use the eight operators below to complete the following two equations.

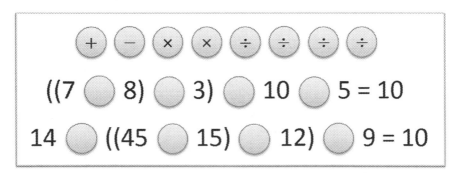

$$((7 \bigcirc 8) \bigcirc 3) \bigcirc 10 \bigcirc 5 = 10$$

$$14 \bigcirc ((45 \bigcirc 15) \bigcirc 12) \bigcirc 9 = 10$$

160

Can you travel from A to B by passing all the white blocks only once each?

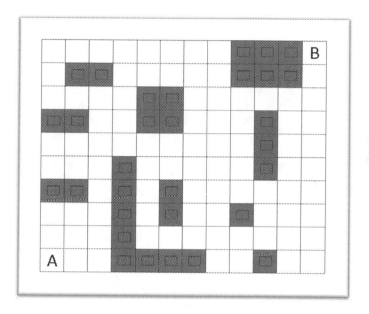

161

Using two straight lines, divide this rectangle into four pieces, each with six flowers.

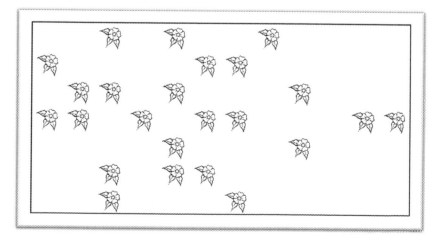

Replace the question marks with + or - so that both diagrams below add up to the same value.

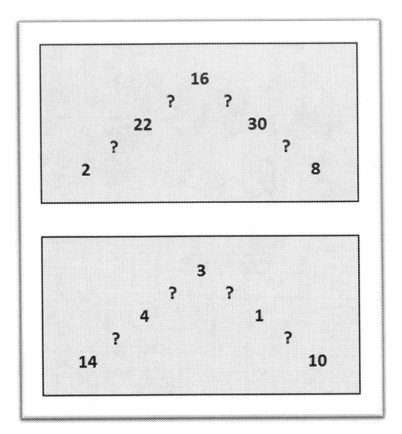

In the following puzzle, starting from any circle, find a twelve-letter English word by going along the lines without crossing any letter more than once.

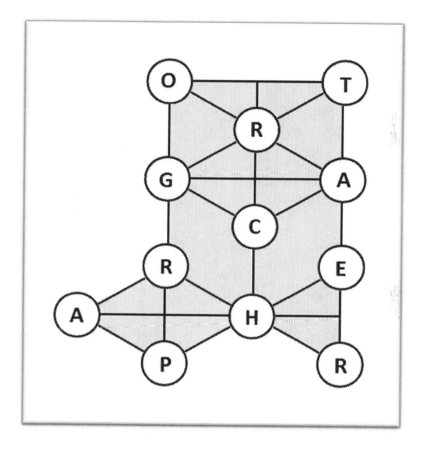

If the following stack of blocks looks the same from the back and front, what is the number of blocks that are used to build it?

If John gets five years older, then the square of his age is increased by 185. How old is John now?

You have only twenty seconds to find out how many times the number 5 is included in the following picture.

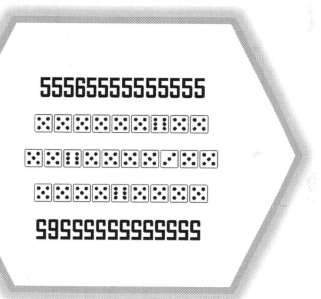

Add three pawns on the following 7×7 board so that there will be only one pawn in any vertical, horizontal, or diagonal line.

168

Steve buys a laptop for $1,270. He pays in cash with a certain number of $5 bills, five times as many $10 bills, a certain number of $50 bills, and twice as many $100 bills. How many bills of each kind does Steve use to pay for the laptop?

Which figure should replace the question mark?

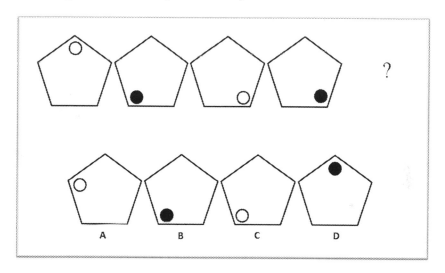

What is the following English word, borrowed from the German?

The following is a 5×5 *Futoshiki* puzzle. Place the numbers 1 to 5 in each row and column such that no number is repeated and the inequality constraints are followed.

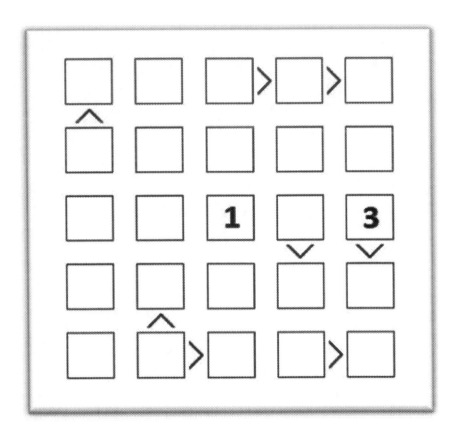

In the following puzzle, starting from any circle, trace out a twelve-letter English word by going along the lines without crossing any letter more than once.

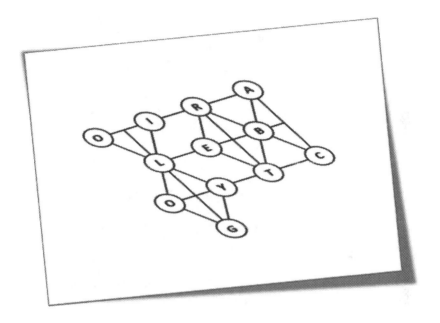

In ten seconds, can you find the four identical abstract flowers?

Draw four intersecting straight lines in order to split the following forty soccer balls into ten groups of four.

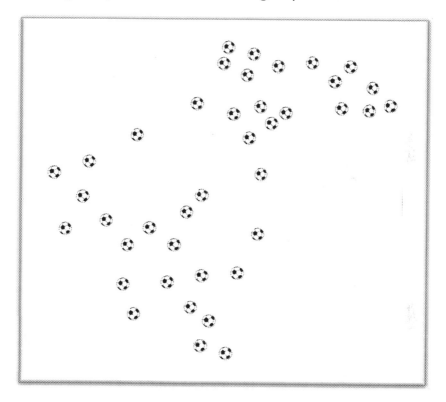

In the following maze, try to connect A to B in five minutes.

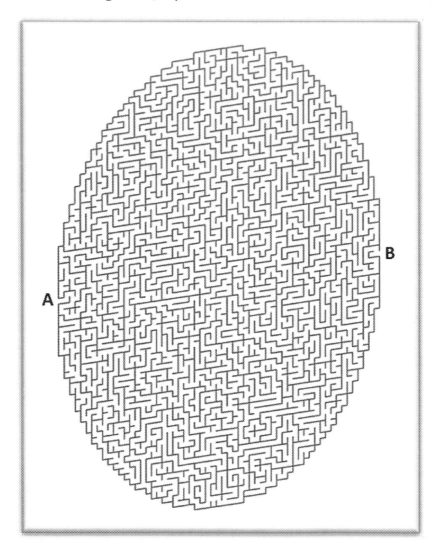

Can you pair up these eight shapes to form four pieces of equal size and shape?

Hint: You do not need to rotate any shapes.

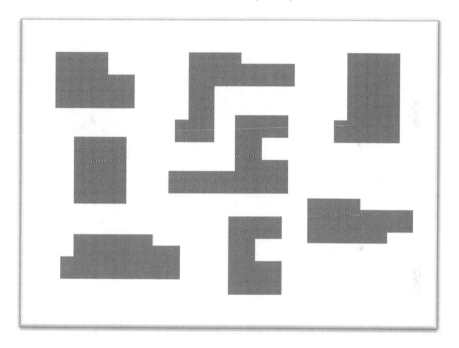

The following nine girls are registered in a makeup school. Try to memorize their faces and figures in no more than thirty seconds.

The new school year starts, and on the second day, a new girl joins the school. In the following picture, without looking at the above picture, can you identify the new girl?

Study the following figure for fifteen seconds.

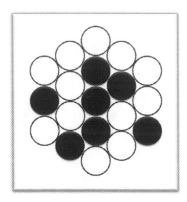

Now, from memory, identify which of the following figures is a rotated copy of the one shown above.

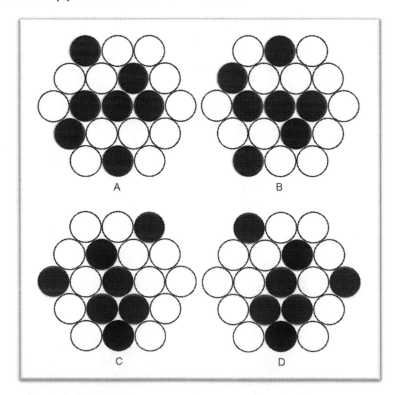

Can you divide the following dark area into six lots with the same shape?

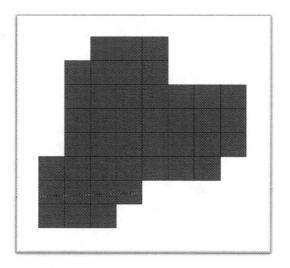

Using two straight lines, divide this heart into four pieces, each of which contains numbers that add up to twenty.

In the following equation, there are nine squares that should contain numbers 1 to 9. Can you find the number of each square?

$$(((\boxed{} \times \boxed{}) \div \boxed{}) \times \boxed{}) - \boxed{} - \boxed{} - \boxed{} = 10$$

Here you will solve ten *Word Fragment Puzzles*. A word fragment puzzle is formed by a clue and an answer, but some letters of the answer are replaced by underscores to represent blank spaces each for a single letter. Example:

To repeat:

   _ _ _emi_ate

The answer is "ingeminate":

$$\underline{i}\ \underline{n}\ \underline{g}\ emi\ \underline{n}\ ate$$

Now try to solve the following word fragment puzzles.

a)   To think:

   _ _ _itat _

b)   To recognize:

   _ _ sce _ _

c)   To fulfill:

_ _ _ om _ lis _

d)   Officially approving:

a _ _ _ oba _ _ _ n

e)   Eating to excess:

_ _ _ let _ _ _

f)   Lackadaisical:

la _ _ _ _ d

g)   Foolishly impractical:

qui _ _ _ i _

h)   To buzz:

_ _ _ bina _ _

i)   Incomprehensible:

_ _ _ cruta _ le

j)   A display of trickery or adroitness:

le _ _ _ de _ ain

In the following puzzle, the numbers 1 to 9 are replaced with nine symbols. Can you identify what value should replace the question mark?

Ω	+	λ	+	Θ	-	Δ	+	Σ	=	17
+		-		+		-		-		
Δ	+	Φ	+	Σ	+	λ	-	Ω	=	8
+		-		+		+		+		
Θ	+	ψ	+	π	+	Ω	-	μ	=	14
-		+		-		-		-		
μ	-	π	+	Φ	+	ψ	-	Δ	=	6
=		=		=		=		=		
7		0		?		4		2		

Look at the following picture, where a piece is missing. Can you identify the missing piece?

In ten minutes, fill in the missing numbers so that each row, each column, and two diagonal lines meet the given totals. Note that numbers must be from 1 to 49, and each number may appear only once.

							159
	31	19		38	43	9	197
32	46		37	5	2		173
	13	36		11	44	10	147
33		20	47		48	27	234
7	21		12	24	1		108
34		3	17		14	28	137
16	22		42	23		45	229
186	198	182	181	136	193	149	261

One of these figures is different from the rest. Can you spot the difference in fifteen seconds?

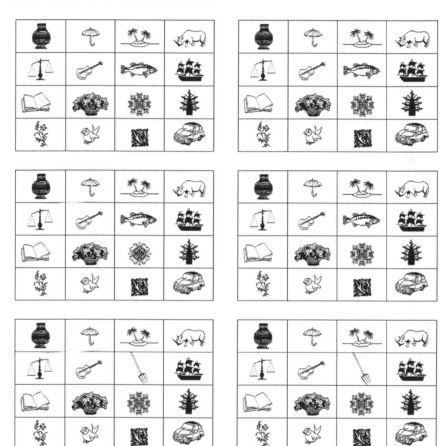

In two minutes, can you form two sets of three identical flowers from the following picture?

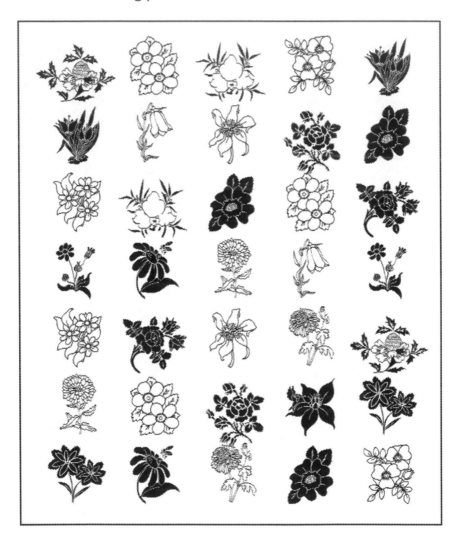

In this word search puzzle, ten Golden Globe Award–winning films are listed. Can you find them?

```
S X R M J L G F W N J L Q V A I Z P M E
N I N R O P P T T I H A C A V P X R N E
Y H R U E E N M E A F W Q Z M E J U D L
G B E A O S Z Z N T P R Z B M O T X A P
N D T J P E H Y A N R E J D K R C Y E O
G Z D F I N F E H U Y N B S O Z Z S N E
M G Y W O V I W N O W C R F O G B H B P
K S G V H R U N I M W E F D C K S I J Y
E A W S T R D N A K K O P O K Y X K U R
N K L L M D T I V C L F M Y O G P T N A
H Z T D J I L M I A I A O L H O N H Y N
V Z O N I Y P L S B Y R X C M C Z E J I
O S X T I V S R S E A A E L V O A W E D
T U Q R N Y E U U K Y B W M U W Q R D R
B F P O T V E Z D O R I W F A Y B E R O
E Z G I E H Y X Z R W A F L P N P S K E
W R C R X R S M T B P Q V M I B A T U A
M A N O N T H E M O O N S C K G A L K Y
D R I V I N G M I S S D A I S Y K E H M
T R A E H E H T N I S E C A L P H R A V
```

An American in Paris

Brokeback Mountain

City Slickers

Driving Miss Daisy

Lawrence of Arabia

Man on the Moon

Ordinary People

Places in the Heart

Reversal of Fortune

The Wrestler

Find one letter in each word below that can be changed to another letter in order to make a new word.

- cheater
- shock
- shore
- chore
- maker

Which word in parentheses is opposite in meaning to the word in capital letters?

PETTY (trivial, matter, important, insignificant, rotator)

Use the eight operators given below to complete the following two equations.

+	+	+	−	—	×	×	÷

$((17 \;\boxed{}\; 18) \;\boxed{}\; (12 \;\boxed{}\; 13)) \;\boxed{}\; 10 = 100$

$10 \;\boxed{}\; (((45 \;\boxed{}\; 9) \;\boxed{}\; 4) \;\boxed{}\; 1) = 100$

In a minute, can you find which of the following figures has the longest perimeter?

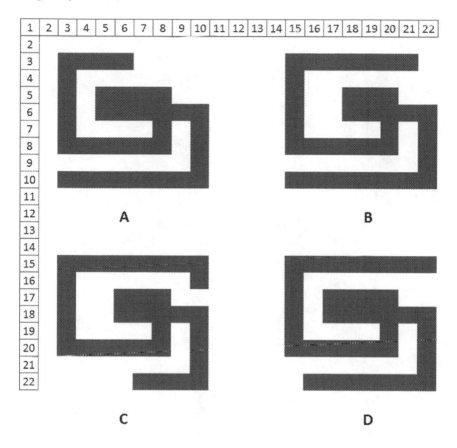

In the following figure, can you find which four figures are identical in twenty seconds?

In this puzzle, there are twelve fish that should be divided by three overlapping circles, each circle containing seven fish. Can you draw the circles?

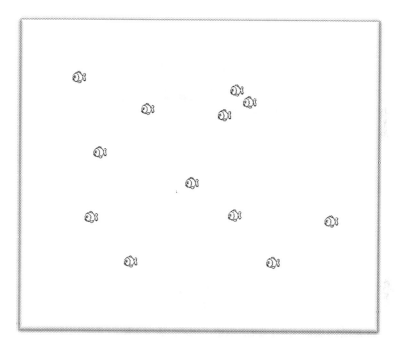

Study this picture for a moment.

In which of the following figures, if a section inside is rotated, would the above picture be found?

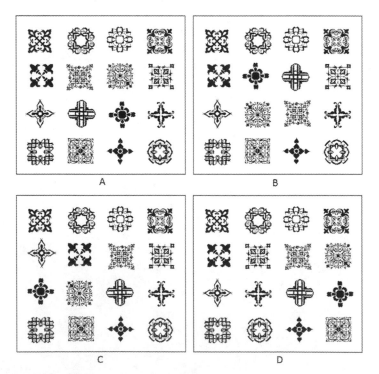

196

This chain of letters below contains the names of three European countries with the letters in the correct order. Try to identify them in two minutes.

FLUPINXOREMLABTONURUGDALG

197

Arrange these twelve boxes into three equal stacks so that the totals of the numbers of the stacks are the same.

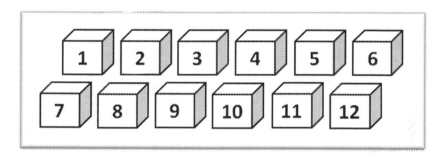

198

Study these four items for twenty seconds; spend only five seconds on each.

Now identify which of the following four pictures contains all four items.

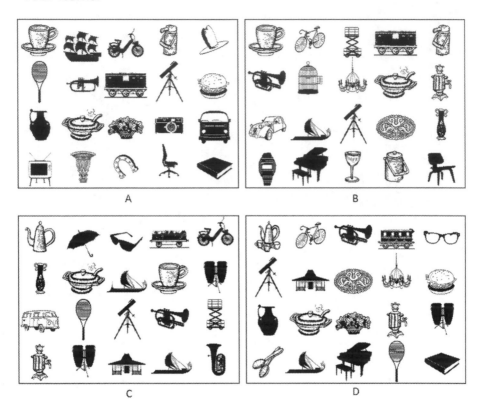

A

B

C

D

199

In the following equation there are nine squares that should contain numbers 1 to 9. Can you find the number of each square?

$$(\square \times \square) + (\square \div \square) + (\square \div \square) - (\square \times \square) = 20$$

200

Simon sold 420 iPads during a six-day sale. Each day he sold twelve more iPads than he did on the previous day. Can you find how many iPads were sold on the last day?

201

Find the number corresponding to each letter in the grid so that the equation is valid.

As an easy memory challenge, study the animal silhouettes that follow for two minutes.

Without looking at the above silhouettes, answer the questions below:

a) How many horses are there?

b) Are there more butterflies than fish?

c) What is the last animal depicted?

d) What is the number of lions?

203

Using two straight lines, divide this circle into four pieces, each of which contains numbers that add up to nineteen.

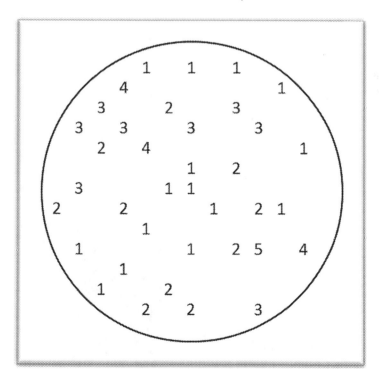

204

The following two grids contain an identical series (i.e., there is a chain of connected squares in each of them). Can you find them in one minute?

C	2	I	6	B	8	J	U
G	H	G	R	7	1	C	5
Y	9	3	F	P	A	6	P
M	9	C	4	N	O	L	G
Y	0	T	5	5	4	8	A
B	R	2	I	S	4	T	D
R	3	Z	A	T	0	1	T
J	2	V	5	9	R	D	E

3	Y	O	Q	5	Z	2	V
G	5	G	R	7	I	5	4
L	K	2	E	P	B	8	P
M	7	C	3	N	L	O	C
T	0	Y	6	5	3	6	B
R	2	I	N	S	4	T	4
A	Z	2	R	2	K	B	O
J	3	W	6	9	R	B	E

205

Start from any letter and trace out an eleven-letter word by going along the grid lines without crossing any joints more than once.

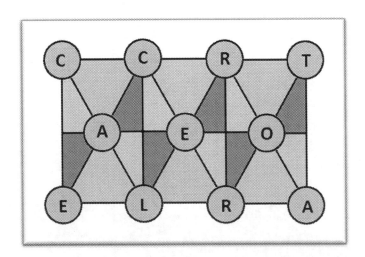

Here is a standard set of twenty-eight dominoes:

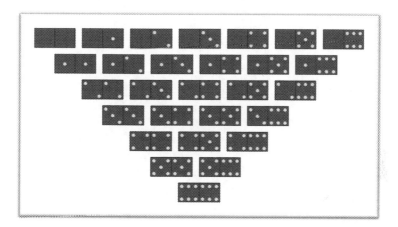

The above dominoes are laid out in the following picture. In three minutes, can you draw all their edges?

As a memory challenge, study the following game board for one minute.

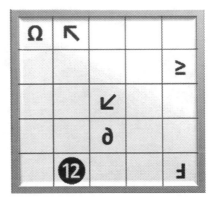

Now, without looking at the above game board, identify which of the following game boards is the exact copy of the above one.

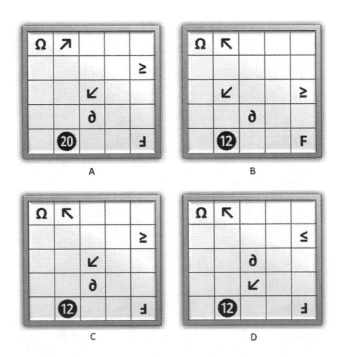

A

B

C

D

What number completes this series?

1   9   19   ?   113

Using only the small figure, while rotating and flipping are allowed, can you form an exact replica of the larger figure?

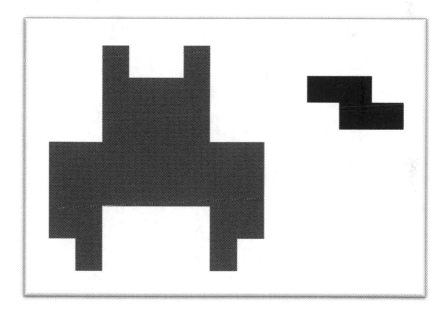

With seven arrows, get a total of 327 points on the following target.

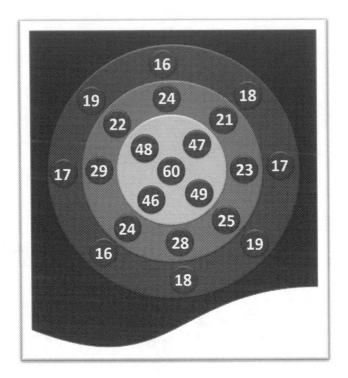

Place the given twelve letters in the star to form four 5-letter words all beginning with B.

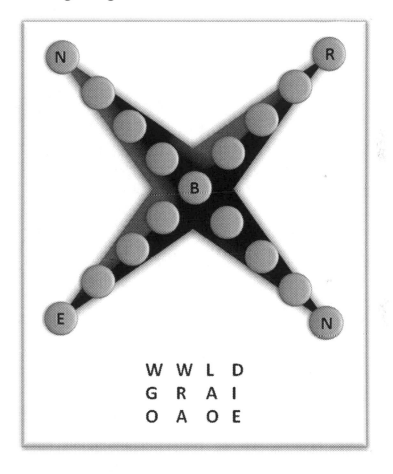

In the following picture, the area of circle B is four times of the area of circle C, and the area of circle D is one unit. How many units is the area of circle A?

a) 64

b) 49

c) 50

d) 100

Hints:
- The area of a circle is π (pi) times the square of the radius: Area = πr2
- The radii of circles A and C are twice the radii of circles B and D, respectively.

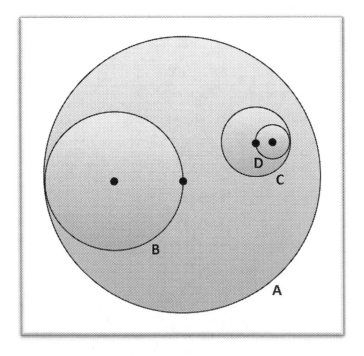

Which of the following strings of letters is the odd one out?

a) SUVXY

b) BNOPL

c) CGPQR

d) MPTVZ

214

Place the numbers 2 to 25 in the cells of the following square so that the sum of the numbers in each row, column, and diagonal is 65.

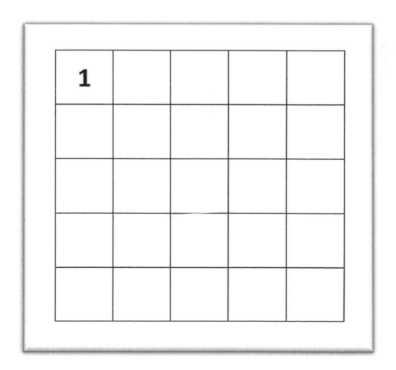

In thirty seconds, can you find which two collections of butterflies are exactly alike?

A

B

C

D

Form two 8-letter words by using the following boxes.

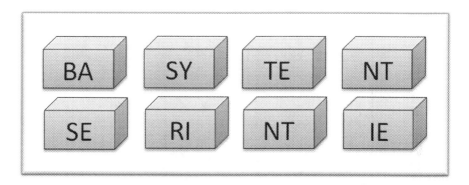

In ten minutes or less, find a path from the START to the END passing only through numbers that are divisible by 12. Note that there is only one solution for this numerical maze.

To make you find numbers divisible by 12 faster, here are three hints to remember and apply:

1. A number is divisible by 12 if it is divisible by 3 *and* 4.

2. If the sum of the digits of a number is divisible by 3, then that number is also divisible by 3. For example, 213 is divisible by 3 because 6, the sum of its digits (2 + 1 + 3 = 6), is divisible by 3.

3. If half of a number is an even number, then that number is divisible by 4. For example, 152 is divisible by 4 because half of it, 76, is an even number. Also, if the last two digits of a number form a number that

is divisible by 4, then the original number is divisible by 4 too. As an example, 732 is divisible by 4 because its last two digits—32—are divisible by 4.

START	36	132	714	654	954	228	830	712	134	922	128
88	914	168	236	258	226	652	468	444	540	58	384
512	382	144	172	851	776	170	732	238	276	190	996
965	918	924	922	455	548	732	996	646	528	452	224
181	784	180	654	892	114	312	196	166	816	900	714
198	782	780	832	224	146	192	412	446	230	456	832
215	88	384	230	540	672	408	658	552	194	192	236
232	715	48	548	228	916	664	995	998	548	708	455
249	694	696	226	348	400	952	254	774	62	840	172
266	296	300	350	924	743	663	144	545	226	240	654
283	944	948	928	732	552	354	568	325	928	168	922
300	163	528	60	396	694	258	444	526	350	648	END

218

Look at the following pattern, where the last row is missing.

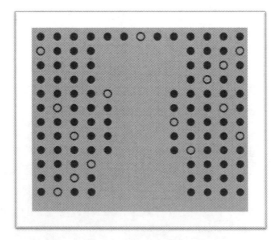

In thirty seconds, can you identify which of the following rows would complete this pattern?

a)

b) ○ ● ● ● ● ● ● ● ○ ● ● ● ● ● ● ●

c) ○ ● ● ● ● ● ● ○ ● ● ● ● ● ● ● ●

d) ● ● ● ● ● ● ● ○ ● ● ● ● ● ● ● ○

219

You have only fifteen seconds to identify which shape in the following picture appears twice.

In one minute, can you arrange the following disks from small to large to make a fifteen-letter English word?

ANSWERS

1

- Scorn
- Salvo
- Salve
- Scope
- Seize

2

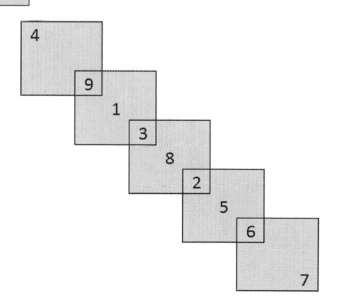

1. Condor
2. Gadwall
3. Surfbird
4. Redstart
5. Dowitcher
6. Spoonbill
7. Nuthatch
8. Shoveler

1	**C**	O	N	D	O	R			
2	G	**A**	D	W	A	L	L		
3	S	U	**R**	F	B	I	R	D	
4		R	E	**D**	S	T	A	R	T
5		D	O	W	**I**	T	C	H	E	R
6		S	P	O	O	**N**	B	I	L	L
7			N	U	T	H	**A**	T	C	H
8			S	H	O	V	E	**L**	E	R

The dark boxes spell out "cardinal."

0

1	+	8	-	2	+	3	=	10
+		+		+		+		
4	+	6	-	5	+	7	=	12
-		-		+		+		
9	+	1	-	2	-	3	=	5
+		-		-		+		
4	-	5	-	6	+	7	=	0
=		=		=		=		
0		8		3		20		

a) False

b) True

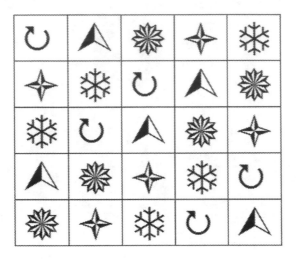

D

a) Conscious

b) Derision

c) Equipment

d) Constituency

e) Sempre

f) Competition

g) Detrimental

h) Misapprehension

i) Inconsiderate

j) Opportunity

11

- Ankara
- Berlin
- Dallas
- Fresno
- Oxford
- Riyadh

12

START	78	312	872	730	800	148	640	76	146	158	86
652	88	546	444	684	842	190	682	118	188	116	562
742	812	160	652	336	830	178	552	108	420	184	676
106	176	104	550	816	164	92	360	112	852	848	196
190	766	252	162	660	118	188	948	136	480	932	790
178	790	834	214	706	142	804	870	124	192	562	442
184	606	858	184	456	306	528	189	130	204	142	212
208	672	854	208	468	556	436	176	978	912	896	754
196	894	972	276	486	164	744	396	648	688	124	194
772	842	190	682	568	188	966	184	110	112	182	142
184	676	112	182	574	176	882	462	96	294	128	574
896	754	824	172	664	100	170	98	196	726	750	END

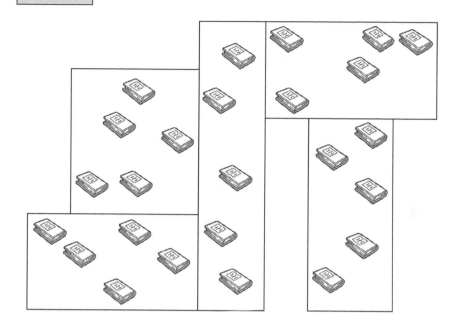

C, D, and L

Indianapolis

D	Q	N	Y	B	E	I	B	E	P	N
U	U	M	G	A	N	U	M	U	A	Y
M	F	X	C	E	R	T	C	M	D	E
H	E	A	B	E	W	M	A	N	A	F
K	C	T	E	O	O	D	I	H	P	J
E	D	O	V	R	I	N	B	L	O	E
M	C	P	H	S	N	C	S	I	B	H
Z	A	D	M	I	G	L	F	M	E	Y
B	E	L	B	O	B	V	E	Y	U	A
P	A	F	G	O	A	L	M	O	C	P
A	C	O	P	D	I	E	E	A	Y	F

16

D

17

Wrangle → Concord

Chapfallen → Cheered

Surcease → Advance

Machination → Honesty

Feeble → Powerful

18

D

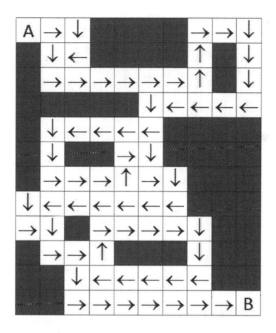

Enlighten

Thenceforth

Editorialized

5	1	3 > 2	4

| 2 | 4 > 1 | 3 | 5 |

| 1 | 3 < 4 < 5 | 2 |

| 3 | 5 | 2 | 4 > 1 |

| 4 | 2 < 5 | 1 | 3 |

22

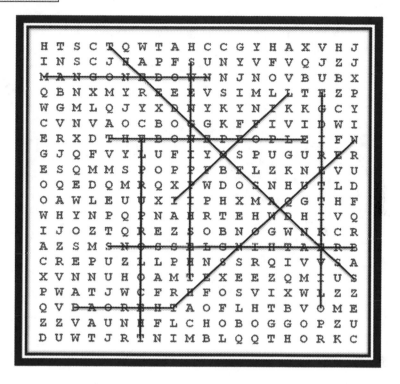

23

$64 (550 + 64 = 614 and 614 + 64 = 678, where the laptop costs $614 and its bag costs $64)

START	G	F	D	L	G	K	U	L	J	D	J
M	O	A	G	I	M	A	Z	A	Q	R	L
Q	T	Z	A	N	G	I	K	U	T	Q	X
U	U	A	B	E	F	F	M	Z	B	A	T
A	J	H	Q	Q	C	I	P	N	O	M	M
N	M	V	P	R	A	N	S	G	F	L	O
X	P	R	U	W	Z	D	T	M	C	J	P
B	E	H	Z	D	A	M	V	P	I	K	K
O	W	I	S	L	F	A	Z	A	E	A	N
J	A	Z	T	H	C	H	W	R	H	Z	A
E	P	A	N	B	Q	R	T	V	W	X	W
P	Y	D	K	M	O	X	A	W	A	Z	END

There are many solutions for this puzzle; the following picture illustrates one:

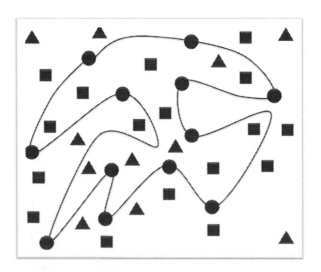

You could make eleven 4-letter words. The following list is a sample answer:

1. BARN
2. FILM
3. TEST
4. YARD
5. COIN
6. GEAR
7. HARD
8. JOKE
9. POST
10. QUAY
11. VIEW

27

3	×	1	−	2	=	1
×		+		−		
5	−	4	+	6	=	7
+		−		×		
9	×	7	−	8	=	55

=　　　=　　　=

24		-2		-46

4	+	11	–	19	+	23	–	14	=	5
×		×		+		+		+		
10	×	3	+	8	–	1	+	21	=	58
–		–		+		+		+		
7	×	24	–	25	–	13	+	6	=	136
–		–		÷		–		+		
12	–	17	–	5	+	15	–	18	=	-13
÷		+		–		+		–		
2	–	22	+	20	×	9	+	16	=	176
=		=		=		=		=		
27		14		12		31		43		

29

Six

30

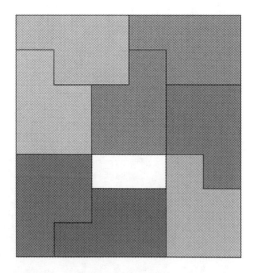

8 + ((9 5 - 3) ÷ 2) - 7 - 1 - 4 6 = 0

a) Summary

b) Volunteer

c) Dormouse

d) Habitat

e) Stronghold

f) Creature

g) Nocturnal

h) Variety

i) Hedgerow

j) Scratch

D, F, N, and S

Nine jobs.

In twelve hours, John, Todd, and Peter can do two, three, and four jobs, respectively.

Ten printers

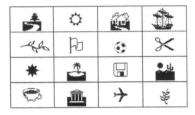

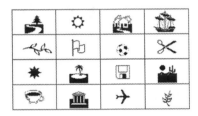

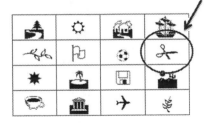

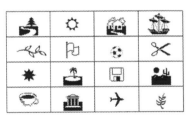

2	4	7	3	■	■	6	8	1	9
0	■	9	7	1	2	3	4	■	6	8
3	2	■	8	6	4	7	5	9	■	0
9	1	8	■	7	5	2	■	8	6	3
1	8	0	7	■	■	1	6	0	9	■
■	9	8	0	5	■	3	2	6	4
1	0	1	■	2	7	6	■	1	9	1
0	■	8	6	9	5	4	3	■	2	0
1	9	■	1	4	2	7	6	8	■	1
4	0	8	7	■	■	9	0	6	2

9

Clockwise, each number is obtained by computing the total of the sums of the digits of the two previous numbers. For example, by having 12 and 12, 6 is obtained: (1 + 2) + (1 + 2) = 6. Hence the question mark should be replaced with 9: (1 + 2) + (6) = 9.

A

Inside the following picture, if the box rotates 180 degrees clockwise, the original picture of this puzzle is found.

C

41

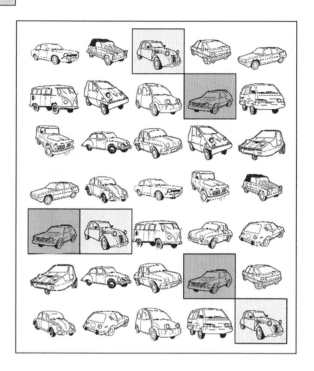

42

1.2, 2.4, 3.6, 4.8, 6

1.2 + 2.4 + 3.6 + 4.8 + 6 = 18

43

- a) Scrutinize & Audit
- b) Convey & Transmit
- c) Quidnunc & Yenta
- d) Excruciation & Harrow
- e) Versatile & Adaptable

44

GREESON
SAYLORVILLE
CRESCENT
WILLIAMSTOWN
BROWN
CANDLEWOOD
CHESUNCOOK
BLACKSHEAR
AUSTIN
BANKSON
CLINTON
BARBEE
CORALVILLE
PILLSBURY
ISTOKPOGA
HARTWICK
KISSIMMEE
WAWASEE
WASHINGTON
SELAWIK
WEDOWEE
NAKNEK
MANITOU
WACONDA
LURLEEN

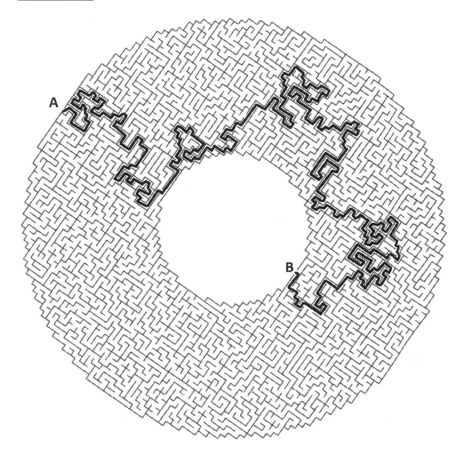

	2	5	6	7		1	3	4
8		9	2		7	4		3
9	4	2		5	3	6	7	
5	3		1	8		9		7
	7	6		4	8	3	1	5
6	5	1	4	3		7		8
3	6		7		2	5	4	
1		7	3	2	6		8	9
7	9		5		4	8		6

47

a) False

b) False

c) True

d) False

e) True

2.

Each term of a Fibonacci sequence is the sum of two preceding terms; that is represented by:

$$F_n = F_{n-1} + F_{n-2}$$

10 $1 bills, 150 $5 bills, 4 $10 bills, and 12 $100 bills

$(10 \times 1) + (150 \times 5) + (4 \times 10) + (12 \times 100) = 10 + 750 + 40 + 1200 = 2000$

1. jewelry

2. keyword

3. mystery

4. rooster

5. benefit

6. clarify

7. fatness

The middle letters of the above words are

ewtsern

By unscrambling ewtsern, WESTERN can be found.

$v = 5$, $w = 4$, $x = 1$, $y = 2$, and $z = 3$

Solution:

$v + w = 9$ → $w = 9 - v$

$w + x = 5$ → $x = 5 - w = 5 - (9 - v) = v - 4$

$x + y = 3$ → $y = 3 - x = 3 - (v - 4) = 7 - v$

$y + z = 5$ → $z = 5 - y = 5 - (7 - v) = v - 2$

As they are positive numbers:

$x > 0$ → $v - 4 > 0$ → $v > 4$

$y > 0$ → $7 - v > 0$ → $v < 7$

As they are whole numbers, v might be 5 or 6. If v is 6, then x will be 2. That is incorrect, as x must be an odd number. Hence, $v = 5$, $w = 4$, $x = 1$, $y = 2$, and $z = 3$.

a) VEXATIOUS & GALLING

b) EREMITE & ANCHORITE

c) BESTOW & CONTRIBUTE

d) SOBRIQUET & EPITHET

e) INEFFABLE & INDESCRIBABLE

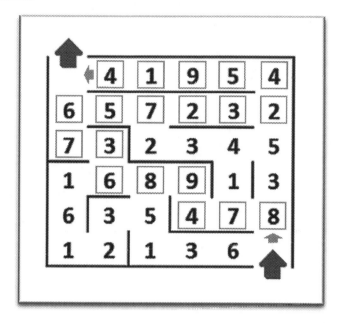

x = 30

y = 25

55

1. Pruning
2. Soil
3. Weeder
4. Scoop

56

A

57

b

58

53

Each letter is connected to 1 plus the alphabetical order of the letter multiplied by 2. For example:

For M, its corresponding number will be:

$1 + [(13) \times 2] = 27$

where M is the letter 13 of the English alphabet.

59

You may recall five bird names out of the following seven ones:

- Gadwall
- Gannet
- Goldeneye
- Grackle
- Grebe
- Grosbeak
- Grouse

60

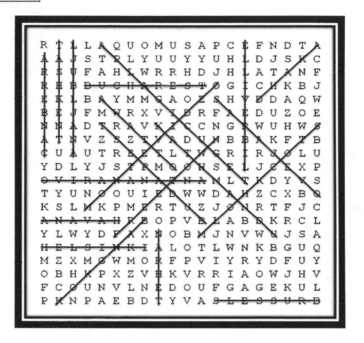

61

START	1	4	13	9	6	16	28	29	15	16	19
2	7	6	1	28	29	30	31	34	35	36	20
4	5	16	26	26	19	4	5	18	10	37	15
7	6	17	33	24	23	45	43	41	40	38	5
9	7	18	17	23	21	48	40	13	20	12	18
11	8	17	19	22	17	49	48	55	36	63	12
20	9	7	14	21	13	51	44	67	68	70	22
19	10	3	16	19	15	55	67	66	3	73	39
23	11	13	8	18	17	57	62	64	6	75	49
5	12	18	10	17	16	8	52	8	87	79	78
11	13	14	15	16	15	18	77	66	77	86	88
18	5	20	14	14	13	74	99	83	84	75	END

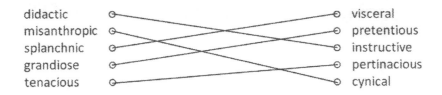

2

8	+	2	+	9	-	3	+	7	=	23
-		-		-		-		-		
3	+	1	+	7	+	2	-	8	=	5
+		+		+		+		+		
9	+	5	+	4	+	8	-	6	=	20
-		-		-		-		-		
6	-	4	+	1	+	5	-	3	=	5
=		=		=		=		=		
8		2		5		4		2		

C, F, M, and P

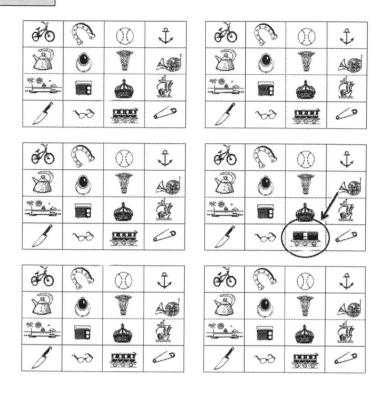

B

From grid to grid, in the first row, each letter moves forward two places in the alphabet.

In the second row, each grid reverses the letters of the previous grid.

In the third row, each letter moves backward one place in the alphabet.

The fourth rows include an English word ending in "est."

B

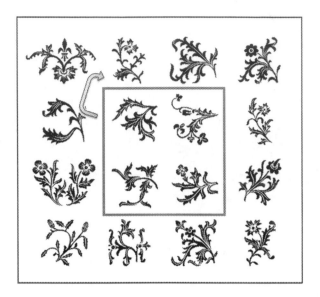

B and C

D

22839 and 45678

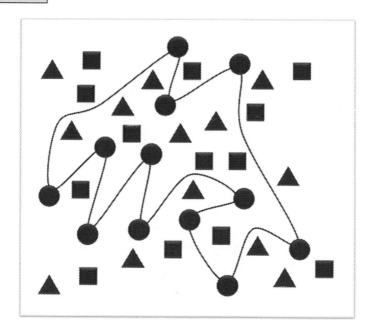

73

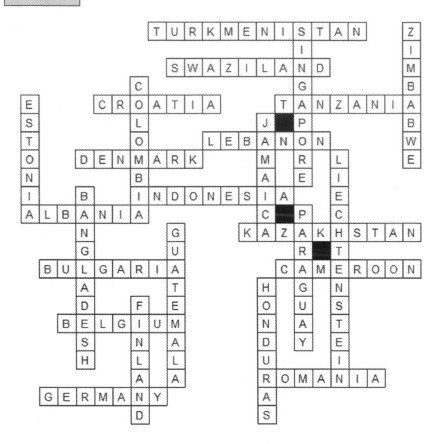

74

a, c, f, and g.

a) 713700 (713700 + 13 = 713713; 713713 ÷ 13 = 54901; hence: 713700 ÷ 13 = 54900)

c) 145158 (145158 − 13 = 145145)

f) 469456 (469456 + 13 = 469469)

g) 363350 (363350 + 13 = 363363)

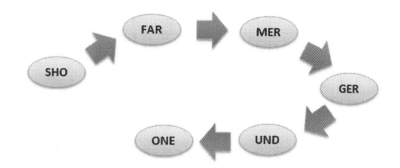

75

1. SHOFAR
2. FARMER
3. MERGER
4. GERUND
5. UNDONE

76

C

77

TRAUMATISM

T	B	M	A
R	A	U	T
K	O	S	I
E	X	M	E

78

7 and 9 (the entire pattern is a palindrome)

79

ADMINISTRATION

80

66 minutes

$66 = (90 \times 11)/(11 + 4)$

81

Five

82

83

a) 6,9,3,20,9,20,9,15,21,19—fictitious

b) 3,25,14,9,3,9,19,13—cynicism

c) 4,9,6,6,21,19,9,2,12,5—diffusible

d) 2,5,1,20,9,20,21,4,5—beatitude

e) 4,9,19,16,15,18,20—disport

f) 6,15,15,12,8,1,18,4,25—foolhardy

g) 8,5,20,5,18,15,13,15,18,16,8,9,3—heteromorphic

h) 4,15,23,14,20,18,15,4,4,5,14—downtrodden

i) 9,14,6,9,18,13,9,20,25—infirmity

j) 9,14,3,9,14,5,18,1,20,5—incinerate

84

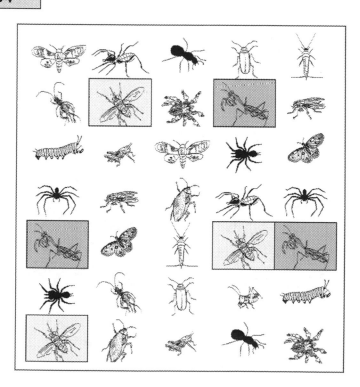

D, H, N, and S

8

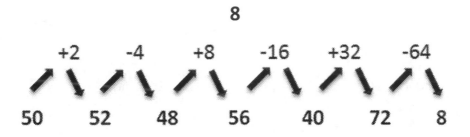

+2   -4   +8   -16   +32   -64

50   52   48   56   40   72   8

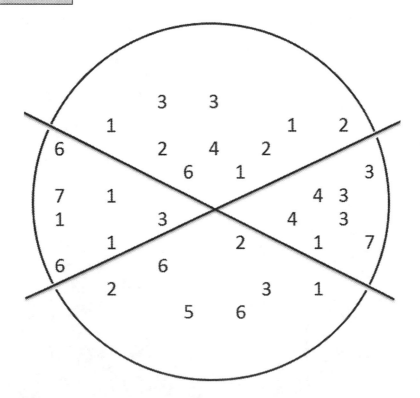

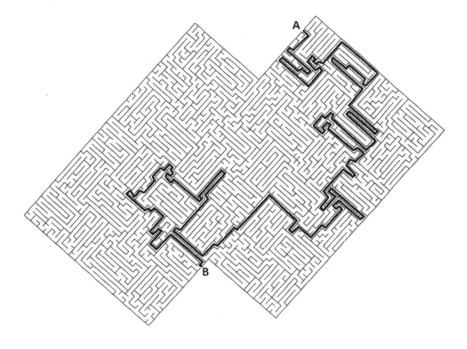

Turn

Twenty circles

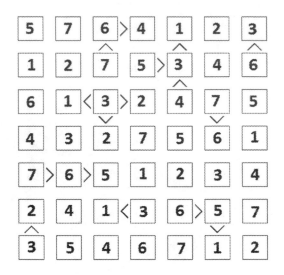

They will not be together in the same corner. Check the following stages, where the dots will be far from each other at the same distance at any stage:

X
60

d + (5) → i (d is the fourth letter and i is the ninth letter)

i + (5) →n

n + (5) →s

s + (5) →x

78 - 3 = 75

75 - 4 = 71

71 - 5 = 66

66 - 6 = 60

94

52 and 62

95

The letter U.

The word is TUTELARY (tutelary means guardian).

1958

for 1958   →   1 + 9 + 5 + 8 = 23

but for the other years:

1955   →   1 + 9 + 5 + 5 = 20

1865   →   1 + 8 + 6 + 5 = 20

1856   →   1 + 8 + 5 + 6 = 20

a) O

b) P

Fore:

Forebear

Forecast

Foregone

17 + 19 - 21 - 13 + 18 = 20

24 - 12 + 16 - 17 + 9 = 20

100

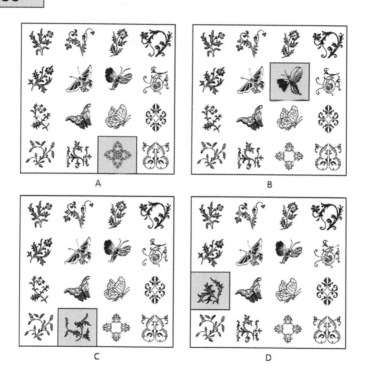

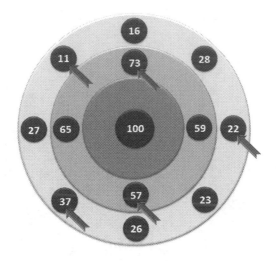

11 + 22 + 37 + 57 + 73 = 200

A

D

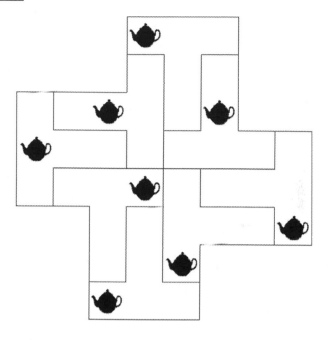

C

106

a) AIRFOIL

b) ALTIMETER

c) PAYLOAD

d) AILERON

e) QUADRIPLANE

107

C. The others are the same figure after rotation.

108

A

109

Eternalize

110

D

D

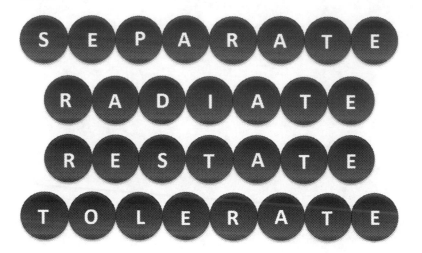

C

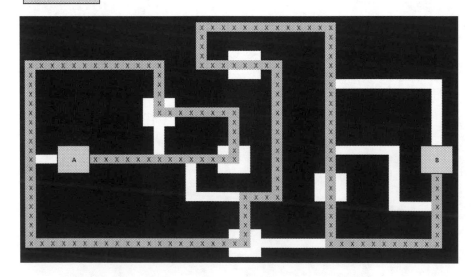

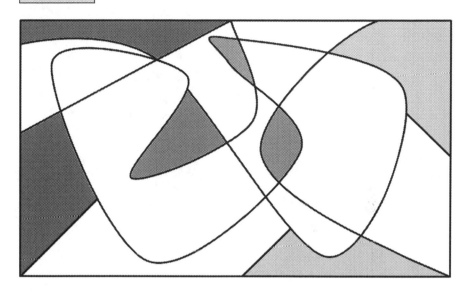

B

a) Cantillation

b) Disinterest

c) Abdominous

d) Adventive

e) Dabchick

Eliminate pins with the numbers 33 and 22 and then group the pins as illustrated below:

41 + 16 + 17 + 24 = 98

21 + 23 + 35 + 19 = 98

17

Solution 1:

9 (green eyes) + 11 (brunettes) + 3 (neither) – 6 (green-eyed brunettes) = 17

Solution 2:

9 – 6 = 3 (green eyes but not brunette)

11 – 6 = 5 (brunette but not green eyes)

3 (neither)

6 (green-eyed brunettes)

3 + 5 + 3 + 6 = 17

1, 3, 4, 7, 8, 9, and 10:

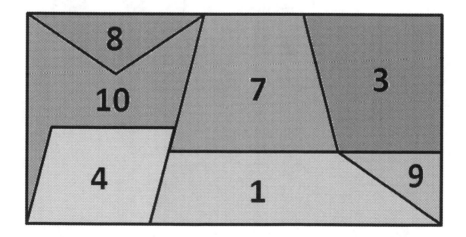

STIPULATE and CONDITION

C

Sixteen times, as illustrated below:

125

Six valves are opened:

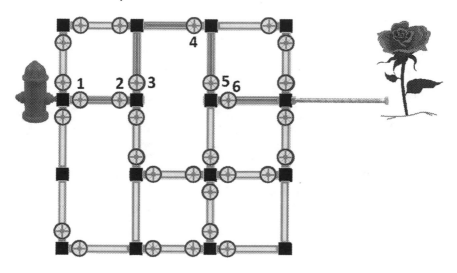

126

ACCOMPLISHED

127

302 [(1 × 2²) + 3, (2 × 3²) + 4, (3 × 4²) + 5, (4 × 5²) + 6, (5 × 6²) + 7, (6 × 7²) + 8]

128

C

129

Z

A → 1

D → 1 + 3 = 4

H → 1 + 3 + 4 = 8

M → 1 + 3 + 4 + 5 = 13

S → 1 + 3 + 4 + 5 + 6 = 19

Z → 1 + 3 + 4 + 5 + 6 + 7= 26

130

You should have drawn the first shape from left.

131

CX

132

B

133

K

23 + 3 = 26 → Z (as Z is the twenty-sixth letter in the English alphabet)

16 + 3 = 19 → S

15 + 3 = 18 → R

8 + 3 = 11 (K is the eleventh letter)

134

17. For each row, the total of the numbers is 40.

135

88 [298 - (1 × 2 × 3), 298 - (2 × 3 × 4), 298 - (3 × 4 × 5), 298 - (4 × 5 × 6), 298 - (5 × 6 × 7)]

136

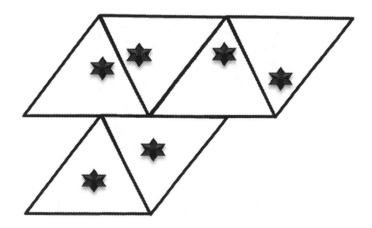

204 and 609

4 + 3 + 2, 9 + 8 + 7, 24 + 23 + 22, 69 + 68 + 67, 204 + 203 + 202, 609 + 608 + 607, 1824 +

69 + 68 + 67 = 204

204 + 203 + 202 = 609

138

144

48 × 3 = 12 × 12 = 144

139

D

99 + 87 + 77 + 7 = 270

33 [119 - 23, 96 - 22, 74 - 21, 53 - 20]

Broccoli

143

117 + 173 + 121 + 129 = 540

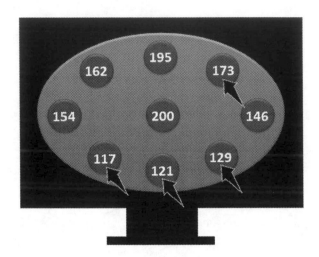

144

h	o	m	o	l	o	g	a	t	e
p	r	o	m	u	l	g	a	t	e
p	r	o	f	l	i	g	a	t	e
c	o	n	g	r	e	g	a	t	e

145

B

First figure: seven edges

Second figure: eight edges

Third figure: nine edges

Fourth figure: ten edges

→ Fifth figure: eleven edges

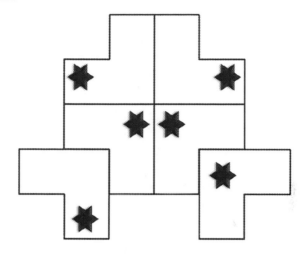

A

D

SINGER (six letters), MACHINE (seven letters), TRAVELER (eight letters), BLISTERED (nine letters)

So the next word should have ten letters.

A) SOLITARY (eight letters)

B) AGREEMENT (nine letters)

C) LEGISLATIVE (eleven letters)

D) CONTIGUOUS (ten letters)

E

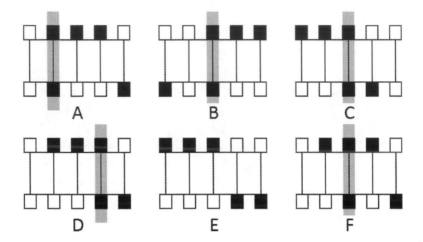

B

A) 42

   series: 72 - 8, 64 - 7, 57 - 6, 51 - 5, 46 - 4

B) 88

   series: 0, 2, 2 × (0 + 2), 2 × (2 + 4), 2 × (4 + 12), 2 × (12 + 32)

C) 65

   series: $1 + 2^1$, $1 + 2^2$, $1 + 2^3$, $1 + 2^4$, $1 + 2^5$, $1 + 2^6$

D) 24

   series: 120 - 21, 99 - 19, 80 - 17, 63 - 15, 48 - 13, 35 - 11

E) 248

series: $0 + 3^0$, $1 + 3^1$, $2 + 3^2$, $3 + 3^3$, $4 + 3^4$, $5 + 3^5$

F) 30

series: $2 \times (9 - 1)$, $2 \times (9 + 2)$, $2 \times (9 - 3)$, $2 \times (9 + 4)$, $2 \times (9 - 5)$, $2 \times (9 + 6)$

152

B. They meet 80 miles from Vancouver and 70 miles from Seattle.

153

b) Eleven days

Every day four meters, but the last day ten meters:

$10 \times (10 - 6) + 10 = 50m$

10 days + 1 last day = 11 days

154

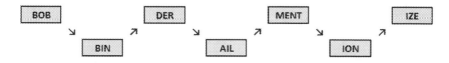

1. BOBBIN
2. BINDER
3. DERAIL
4. AILMENT
5. MENTION
6. IONIZE

Four squares

- Woodpecker
- Flamingo
- Blackbird
- Pheasant
- Bobwhite

a) Thirty words

b) The letter T

c) 14 percent

d) The letters H, K, and X

e) The letters B and F

Jocund → Gloomy

Chicanery → Honesty

Propitious → Inauspicious

Pecuniary → Noncommercial

Vexatious → Pleasing

$((7 + 8) \div 3) \times 10 \div 5 = 10$

$14 - ((45 \div 15) \times 12) \div 9 = 10$

160

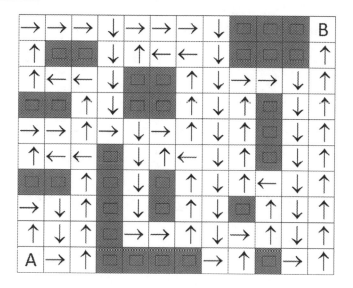

161

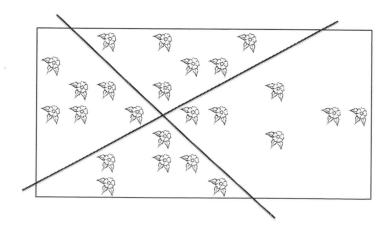

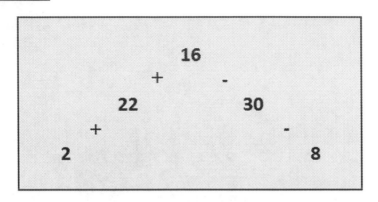

Cartographer (one who makes maps or charts)

Seventy

Sixteen years old

Solution:

x is John's age:

$x^2 + 185 = (x + 5)^2$

$x^2 + 185 = x^2 + 25 + 10x$

$185 - 25 = 10x$

$160 = 10x$

$x = 16$

166

There are fifty number fives in the picture.

167

Fourteen $5 bills, seventy $10 bills, two $50 bills, and four $100 bills

(14 * 5) + (70 * 10) + (2 * 50) + (4 * 100) = 70 + 700 + 100 + 400 = 1,270

C

The dot moves round inside the pentagon 3, 4, 5 places clockwise at each stage and alternates black/white.

Weltschmerz (melancholy at the evils of the world)

3	4	5 > 2 > 1

```
 3    4    5 > 2 > 1
 ^
 4    2    3    1    5

 2    5    1    4    3
                v    v
 5    1    4    3    2
      ^
 1    3 > 2    5 > 4
```

Bacteriology

173

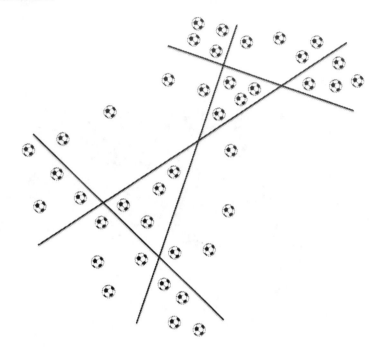

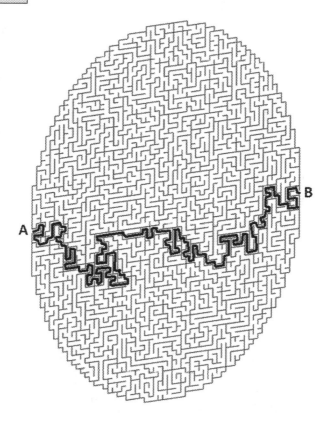

175

176

B

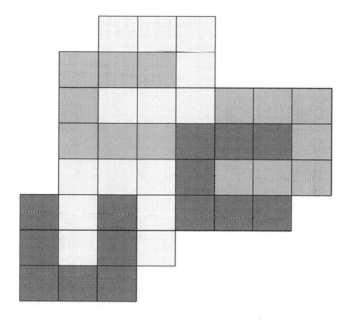

(((1 2 × 3) ÷ 4) × 9) - 5 6 - 7 - 8 = 10

a) Cogitate

b) Discern

c) Accomplish

d) Approbation

e) Repletion

f) Languid

g) Quixotic

h) Bombinate

i) Inscrutable

j) Legerdemain

12

9	+	3	+	1	-	4	+	8	=	17
+		-		+		-		-		
4	+	2	+	8	+	3	-	9	=	8
+		-		+		+		+		
1	+	6	+	5	+	9	-	7	=	14
-		+		-		-		-		
7	-	5	+	2	+	6	-	4	=	6
=		=		=		=		=		
7		0		12		4		2		

184

D

185

49	31	19	8	38	43	9
32	46	25	37	5	2	26
15	13	36	18	11	44	10
33	30	20	47	29	48	27
7	21	39	12	24	1	4
34	35	3	17	6	14	28
16	22	40	42	23	41	45

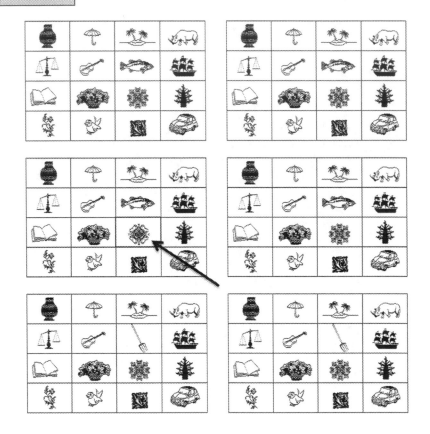

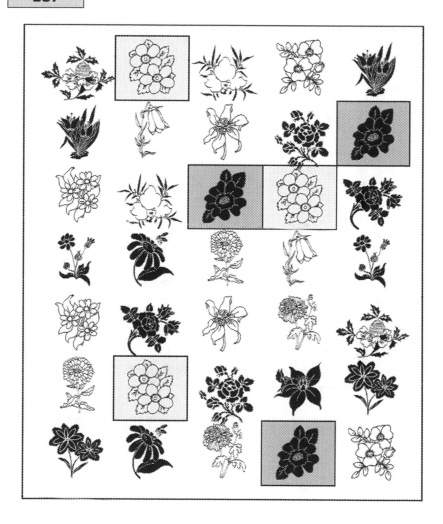

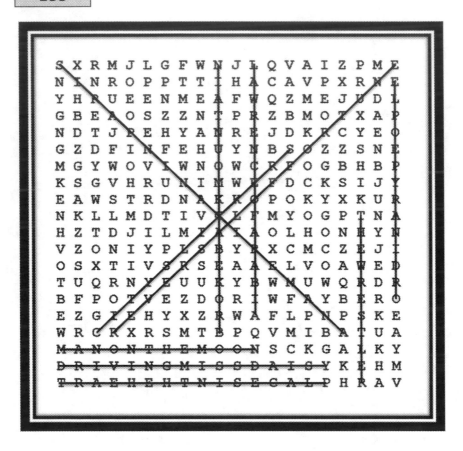

There is more than one solution for this puzzle; the following list provides one of them:

- theater
- shack
- share
- chare (a narrow street)
- mazer

190

Important

191

((17 + 18) - (12 + 13)) × 10 = 100

10 × (((45 - 9) ÷ 4) + 1) = 100

192

D

193

H, I, O, and Q

194

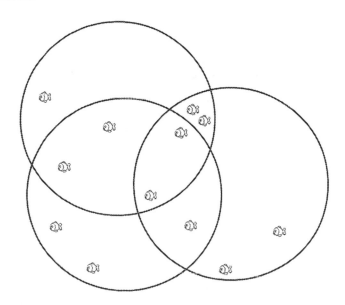

C:

Finland, Luxembourg, and Portugal

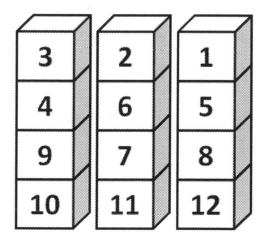

D

($\boxed{4} \times \boxed{5}$) + ($\boxed{9} \div \boxed{3}$) + ($\boxed{8} \div \boxed{2}$) - ($\boxed{1} \times \boxed{7}$) = 20

One hundred iPads

Solution:

6x - 180 = 420 → x = 100

because:

(x - 60) + (x - 48) + (x - 36) + (x - 24) + (x - 12) + x = 420

6	2	5	9	2
3	8	7	0	4

1	0	1	2	9	6

a) Four

b) No

c) Elephant

d) One

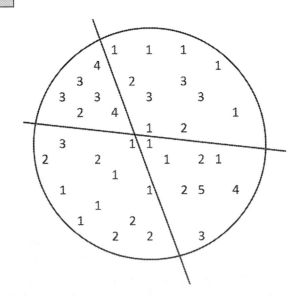

204

C	2	I	6	B	8	J	U
G	H	G	R	7	1	C	5
Y	9	3	F	P	A	6	P
M	9	C	4	N	O	L	G
Y	0	T	5	5	4	8	A
B	R	2	I	S	4	T	D
R	3	Z	A	T	0	1	T
J	2	V	5	9	R	D	E

3	Y	O	Q	5	Z	2	V
G	5	G	R	7	I	5	4
L	K	2	E	P	B	8	P
M	7	C	3	N	L	O	C
T	0	Y	6	5	3	6	B
R	2	I	N	S	4	T	4
A	Z	2	R	2	K	B	O
J	3	W	6	9	R	B	E

205

ACCELERATOR

206

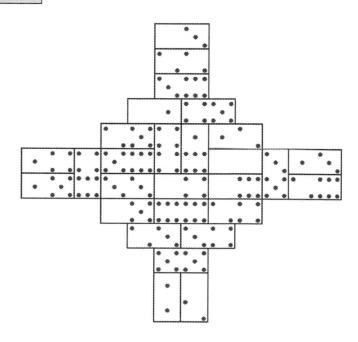

C

47

1	9	19	?	113
		1 + (2 × 9)	9 + (2 × 19)	19 + (2 × 47)

The following figure illustrates one of the possible combinations to get 327 points:

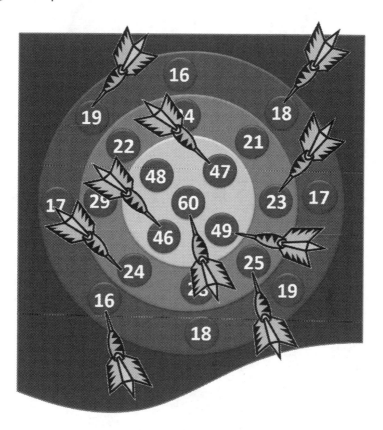

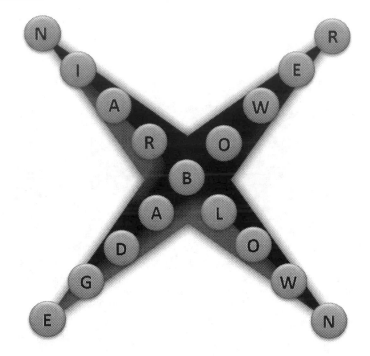

- Brain
- Blown
- Bower
- Badge

a) 64

The area of circle A is four times of the area of circle B, and the radius of circle A is twice that of circle B. The area of circle B is four times the area of circle C, and the area of circle C is four times of the area of circle D ($4 \times 4 \times 4 = 64$).

213

b (In the other strings, letters are in alphabetically ascending order.)

214

1	2	20	23	19
3	25	4	12	21
22	18	13	5	7
24	6	11	16	8
15	14	17	9	10

215

B & D

216

SENTIENT & SYBARITE

START	36	132	714	654	954	228	830	712	134	922	128
88	914	168	236	258	226	652	468	444	540	58	384
512	382	144	172	851	776	170	732	238	276	190	996
965	918	924	922	455	548	732	996	646	528	452	224
181	784	180	654	892	114	312	196	166	816	900	714
198	782	780	832	224	146	192	412	446	230	456	832
215	88	384	230	540	672	408	658	552	194	192	236
232	715	48	548	228	916	664	995	998	548	708	455
249	694	696	226	348	400	952	254	774	62	840	172
266	296	300	350	924	743	663	144	545	226	240	654
283	944	948	928	732	552	354	568	325	928	168	922
300	163	528	60	396	694	258	444	526	350	648	END

217

218

b

Note that in the whole pattern, there are six black disks between each pair of subsequent white ones.

220

PULCHRITUDINOUS

Pulchritudinous means "having great physical beauty or appeal."